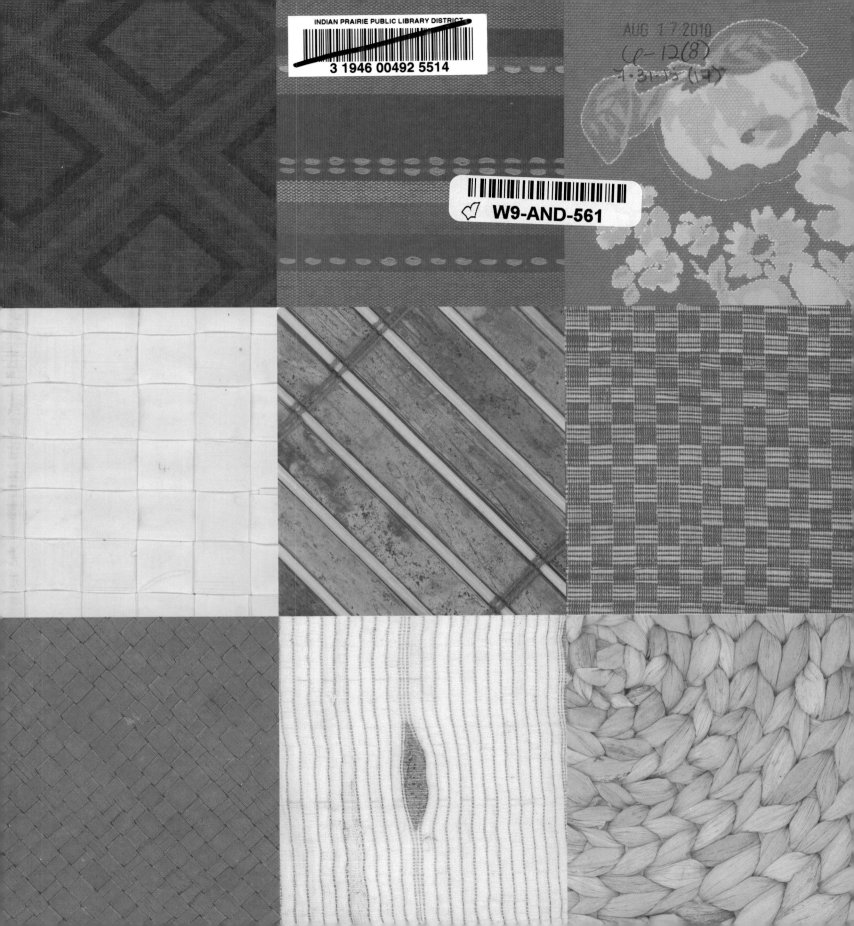

The Filipino-American Kitchen

TRADITIONAL RECIPES
CONTEMPORARY FLAVORS

JENNIFER M. ARANAS

PHOTOGRAPHS BY

BRIAN BRIGGS & MICHAEL LANDE

TUTTLE PUBLISHING

Tokyo · Rutland, Vermont · Singapore

For Mom, who gave me this amazing cuisine, and for Cesar and Lena, who feed my spirit every day.

Published by Tuttle Publishing, an imprint of Periplus Editions (HK) Ltd., with editorial offices at 364 Innovation Drive, North Clarendon, Vermont 05759.

Text © 2006 Jennifer M. Aranas
Photography © 2006 Periplus Editions (HK) Ltd.

Library of Congress Cataloging-in-Publication Data
Aranas, Jennifer M., 1970–
  The Filipino-American kitchen: traditional recipes, contemporary flavors / Jennifer M. Aranas.
  p. cm.
  ISBN 0-8048-3836-4 (hardcover : alk. paper)
1. Cookery, Philippine. 2. Filipino Americans—Food. I. Title.
  TX724.5.P5A73 2006
  641.59599—dc22
                         2006013387
ISBN-10: 0-8048-3836-4
ISBN-13: 978-0-8048-3836-8

Distributed by
North America, Latin America & Europe
Tuttle Publishing, 364 Innovation Drive
North Clarendon, VT 05759-9436
Tel: (802) 773-8930 Fax: (802) 773-6993
info@tuttlepublishing.com www.tuttlepublishing.com

Asia Pacific
Berkeley Books Pte. Ltd., 130 Joo Seng Road
#06-01 Singapore 368357
Tel: (65) 6280-1330 Fax: (65) 6280-6290
inquiries@periplus.com.sg www.periplus.com

First edition   10 09 08 07   10 9 8 7 6 5 4 3 2

Printed in Singapore

CONTENTS

GROWING UP IN A FILIPINO-AMERICAN KITCHEN

The Filipino-American Kitchen is a book about enjoying Filipino food the way I grew up enjoying it, separated by oceans and continents from the lush Philippine Islands yet with a heart filled with Filipino spirit and tradition. I was born and raised in Chicago, halfway around the globe from the island of Cebu, where a russet sun shone over my parents' general store as they sold kilos of rice and refreshing glasses of *halo-halo* to nursing students at the nearby university. When they sold their store and moved to the United States in the late 1960s, they brought with them traditions of language, religion, and food that sustained them in their new home. For my sister, brother, and me, those customs translated into a household where both English and Visaya were spoken, where Sunday mornings were reserved for church, and the kitchen was the heart of our home.

I had the tremendous privilege of being born into a family of excellent cooks, which meant that everyday meals were as delicious and lovingly prepared as the fiesta dishes offered at family celebrations. It also meant that kitchen shortcuts were not the standard. For example, coconut did not come pulverized and presweetened in a bag nor did coconut milk come in a can. Around the same age that I learned how to ride a bike, my grandfather taught me how to properly shred a coconut "homestyle" on a short wooden bench fitted with a round, serrated metal blade. My mother then soaked the shredded meat in water and squeezed it to extract coconut milk for *guinataan,* a savory coconut soup, or reduced the milk on the stovetop into *latik,* a thick cream spread on cassava cake. The squeezed, shredded coconut meat was dried or toasted for sweetened rice cakes. In setting high culinary standards, my family taught me the principles of quality, flavor, texture, and balance that set Filipino food apart as a satisfying and memorable cuisine.

My husband and I spent the better part of our twenties and thirties serving long tours of duty deep in the trenches of the restaurant industry—me in the back of the house, cooking, and he in the front. Fine-dining French, Italian, American, contemporary, and Pan-Asian restaurants were our training ground, allowing us to work our way through the kitchens and dining rooms of Europe and Asia without ever leaving U.S. soil. When we decided to open Rambutan in 1998, there was no question in my mind that the menu was going to feature the Filipino food of my heart. Although I was certain that most of the nearly 4 million Chicagoans had no notion what Filipino food was about, I longed to share the cuisine that my childhood and years of professional training had prepared me for—the flavors of Southeast Asia and the techniques of Europe combined in one kitchen.

Rambutan wasn't the first Filipino restaurant in Chicago. A handful of brave pioneers already ran Filipino eateries that were northside mainstays. But what I wanted for my own place was a cuisine that reflected my roots while embracing my American upbringing. It meant serving traditional Filipino cuisine that included the wonderfully fresh and vibrant ingredients available locally. Thus, the culinary doors were flung open to endless possibilities. *Adobo,* a Filipino national dish, was no longer just for pork or chicken when Maple Leaf Farms, a local duck farm, sold fresh duck right across the border in Indiana. I could, without guilt, forgo frozen *bangus* (milkfish) for fresh day-boat Lake Superior whitefish. Never again did I have to open a can of *Ligo* sardines to make *misua* soup when my fish purveyor delivered fresh sardines within forty-eight hours of being caught. And tomato-cucumber salad could be easily completed by the addition of Wisconsin buffalo mozzarella instead of the native caribou cheese, *kesong puti*. That is how both my restaurant and this book were born—out of a deep respect for my native cuisine alongside an understanding of American dining and a desire to use fresh local products.

Jennifer M. Aranas

The roots of Filipino-American cuisine lie in one of the world's first culinary melting pots, the Philippines—an archipelago of several thousand islands that borders the Philippine Sea on the east, the South China Sea on the west, and the Celebes Sea on the south. A country of Malay origin, the Philippines is largely a product of deep impressions made by Spanish and American conquerors. Prior to Western colonization, the islands were inhabited by a Malay population scattered throughout the archipelago. Having established a relationship with the natives early in the ninth century, the Chinese became their primary trading partner establishing a strong commercial and social presence on the islands. Arab, Indian, Portuguese, and Japanese traders followed suit, making the islands an important trading port where silver, spices, commodities, and wares exchanged hands.

Sailing under the Spanish flag of King Charles V, Portuguese explorer Ferdinand Magellan set foot on the Pacific island of Samar in 1521. But it wasn't until a subsequent expedition in 1542 that Ruy Lopez de Villalobos gave a name to the islands calling them "Filipinas" after the crown prince of Spain, Philip II. The first Spanish colony, established in 1565, began 334 years of colonizing and Catholicizing the Philippines, erasing much of their native culture and religion. However, the conquistadores were not completely without merit, having funneled to the islands important economic crops and livestock from New Spain (their Mexican territories), such as avocado, cacao, tomatoes, maize, and cattle.

The era of Spanish rule came to a halt with the Treaty of Paris in 1898, which ended the Spanish-American war and ceded the Philippines, along with Cuba, Guam, and Puerto Rico, to the United States. U.S. President William McKinley wasted no time developing the Philippines' social and economic infrastructure in the American exemplar, spreading English and ideals of democracy all over the islands. Having spent forty-seven years grooming the Philippines for its freedom, the United States granted the Philippines independence in 1946.

The Original Fusion Cuisine
It is hard to resist the vibrant flavors of ginger and lemongrass, the glorious triumvirate we lovingly call *sofrito* (sautéed onion, garlic, and tomato), or the crispy crunch of egg rolls in various incarnations. On the surface, Filipino food is entirely familiar. Noodles, rice, stews, and stir-fries are neither new nor Filipino inventions. But the interplay of exotic flavors, balanced and harmonious, is uniquely Filipino and anything but ordinary.

Filipino history explains the motley of influences on the Philippines' simple food. Modern Filipino cuisine is a collage of ethnicities starting with a native Malay base flavored with layers of Chinese, Spanish, and American accents. Rice is a longtime staple in the Philippines, having been cultivated since 3200 B.C.E., and today is still unequivocally the primary food. Dishes heavily laden with coconut (*guinataan*, for example) or vinegar (stewed *paksiw*, raw *kinilaw*, and pickled *achara*) are attributed to the Malay natives. Fermented fish and shrimp pastes are used to season raw and cooked foods from green mangoes and sliced bitter melon to *kare-kare*, oxtail in peanut sauce, and *pinakbet*, vegetable stew. Dishes such as *inasal*, grilled or roasted meats, *sinigang*, sour soups, *bachoy* and *bopiz*, stewed organ meats, *tinutungan*, chicken with palm hearts, *tapa*, marinated dried beef, and *dinuguan*, pig's blood stew, exemplify the simple, varied, and original style and flavor of the Islands.

Chinese traders who established themselves in the Philippines early in the ninth century contributed significantly to Filipino cuisine with a large variety of noodles (*pancit*), steamed buns and dumplings (*siopao* and shumai*), and egg rolls (*lumpia*). *Arroz caldo*, *pospas*, and *lugaw* are Filipino adaptations of Chinese congee. Soy sauce, ginger, tofu, fermented black beans, and dried mushrooms are all Chinese flavors commonly found in Filipino food.

The Spanish, who conquered the Islands in 1542 left the deepest impressions on Filipino cuisine by integrating their homeland foods, renaming native dishes in Spanish, and importing New World flavors from Mexico, their North American territory through which the islands were governed. Spanish colonists taught their Filipino cooks how to prepare such favorite homeland dishes as *caldereta* beef stew, meat-filled empanadas, meat and chickpea *cocido*, chicken pastel, savory egg-based tortillas, and paellas—all cooked and flavored so differently than the steamed, white rice of the Islands. Quickly cooking a *sofrito* of tomato, garlic, and onion in olive oil is the flavor base that preludes many Filipino sautéed dishes (*guidsdos*). Other dishes that bear Spanish ancestry are *almondigas* (meatballs), *sopa de ajo* (garlic soup), *morcon* (stuffed beef roll), and croquettes (savory fritters). Desserts are overwhelmingly European in style, replete with rich custards and buttery cakes. Flan (egg custard), *natillas* (soft cream custard), *brazo de mercedes* (meringue jelly roll), *budin* (bread pudding), *mazapan* (marzipan), *turron* (nut nougat), *capuchinos* (brandy-soaked cakes), and *buñuelos* and *churros* (fried dough fritters) were indulgent endings to Spanish meals served with coffee or hot chocolate, a practice still relished today.

The Mexican influence on Filipino cuisine may not be apparent on the surface because it was indirectly introduced secondhand through the Spanish. But today, crops from Mexico are an integral component of a modern Philippines. From a culinary standpoint, Mexico's food is not so obvious; tacos, burritos, enchiladas, and fajitas never made the journey across the Atlantic Ocean nor did the New World's abundant supply of chiles. More subtle dishes such as tamales, *menudo*, and *pipían* were brought to the islands along with native ingredients such as tomato, chayote, avocado, squash, annatto seeds, and cacao. Among the most consequential commodities introduced to the islands was maize, which now ranks as the second most important crop in the Philippines behind rice. Corn is vital not only as a human food staple but as livestock feed and processed commercial products.

When the United States was ceded the Philippines following the Treaty of Paris, thus began nearly fifty years of American military occupation that integrated quintessential American foods like SPAM, macaroni salad, hot dogs, and hamburgers into everyday Filipino fare. Filipinos were quick to embrace these new foods and equally eager to adapt them to their palates. Fried chicken is first marinated in soy, garlic, and bay leaves; spaghetti sauce is made sweet with just a touch of sugar; canned corned beef is sautéed with garlic, onion, and tomato; meat loaf is made with ground pork and studded with chorizo, olives, and raisins; hamburgers and fries are spread with banana ketchup. Though the Spanish reigned longer over the Philippines than other conquerors, American President William McKinley integrated a program of Americanism that remains strong today.

In an independent Philippines, what does nearly half a millennium of western colonialism combined with Asian geography amount to today? A fiesta buffet that is the truest of cultural crossroads, a fantastic spread filled with dishes from Malaysia, Spain, China, Mexico, and the United States, yet all made Filipino style.

Enjoying a Filipino Meal

Different from the Western custom of serving meals in courses, Filipinos place equal importance on each dish, bringing them all—from soup to salad to entrées and desserts—to the table at the same time. The focus of every meal—breakfast, lunch, or dinner—is rice. Everything else, from the soup to the viand to the vegetable is a rice "topping." Other toppings include an assortment of condiments and dipping sauces such as vinegar with soy and garlic, chile peppers with *calamansi*, or fish sauce with ginger placed on the table for the diner to individually season his food to his own liking. Eating is done with a spoon and fork in which the back of the fork is used to push a combination of rice, meat, vegetable, and sauce onto the spoon creating the perfect bite.

Breakfast, lunch, and dinner are the main meals throughout the day. *Meriendas* are also traditionally enjoyed, though busy schedules are quickly making this practice extinct. Merienda is the repose of a midmorning or midafternoon refreshment, which can be a snack of bread and coffee or a more substantial taking of *ukoy* shrimp fritters or tamales. Offerings are light, which means that steamed white rice is usually not on the menu. Yet, the importance of rice in Filipino cuisine could not preclude it from being included in various forms: sweet rice cakes (*bibinka*, *puto*), wrapped rice snacks (*suman*), and hearty rice porridge (*champorado* and *arroz caldo*) are among the many choices for merienda fare.

With the emphasis on food in *The Filipino-American Kitchen*, it's easy to neglect Filipino beverages. Native drinks are plentiful. Natural fruit juices are ubiquitous throughout the Islands. Mango, guava, pineapple, young coconut water, and calamansi are among the endless variety of fruits transformed into pure, refreshing nectars. Despite the long relationship with China, the art of tea drinking was not a widespread tradition in the Philippines. However, hot fruit teas such as calamansi tea or *salabat* ginger tea are common beverages as are American-style iced teas. The Philippines was emphatically receptive to the Spanish's coffee culture. Coffee and hot chocolate are the beverages of choice paired with breakfast, merienda, or after-dinner dessert.

Filipinos are also fond of their alcoholic libations. Grape wines are nearly nonexistent but replaced instead with native wines creatively made from local resources. *Tuba* is the pervasive wine fermented from the sap of palm tree buds. Coconut palm sap is the superior choice although buri, nipa, and sugar palms are all viable sources of sap. *Tapuy* and *pangasi* are the most common wines made from rice or corn. The sugarcane wine *basi* traces its roots to the province of Ilocos Norte located on the northern tip of Luzon. It is amber-colored and flavored with the bark of fragrant trees such as *samak* or *kabarawan*. Fruit wines include plum wine called *duhat* or *lomboy* and mango wine. Distilled spirits include *layaw*, a potent corn distillation and *lambanog*, a distilled version of *tuba*. *Anisado* is similar to *lambanog* but lightly flavored with anise seeds. And, of course, there's beer. San Miguel is the official Filipino brand.

As with any cuisine, the best way to enjoy a meal is with a beverage that complements the food. With its emphasis on seafood and poultry and tart flavors, Filipino cuisine lends itself to the enjoyment of light-bodied alcoholic beverages—such as lagers, pilsners, and pale ales, and fruity white wines such as Riesling or Gewurztraminer. There are exceptions, of course, for the heavier beef, lamb, or poultry dishes. For example, duck braised in adobo with pineapple and tomatoes pairs well with a fruity, weighty merlot and cashew-crusted lamb is best washed down with a nutty, medium-bodied dunkel. So although the rule to food and beverage pairings is that there are no rules, matching comparable flavors will steer you in the right direction to find the perfect potation for your meal.

The Recipes

What you'll find in *The Filipino-American Kitchen* is a refreshing mix of Filipino old world and new. Traditional recipes come straight from the islands, adjusted marginally to account for native ingredients that are normally used fresh in the Philippines but that may only be offered in a preserved state here. I've also compiled traditionally based recipes bursting with the flavors of the Philippines but modified to include the bounty of fresh meat, fish, and vegetables offered in the United States. These are dishes that reveal my American fingerprint, which would not normally appear at a traditional Filipino meal, yet maintain the integrity of Filipino flavor, style, and technique.

Although many of the recipes in *The Filipino-American Kitchen* found their way onto my restaurant's menu, this is not a restaurant cookbook. The recipes don't require culinary school graduates to prepare, cook, and meticulously plate each dish. This is everyday food. In my house, quick meals, regardless of ethnicity, take as much priority as healthy, delicious ones. Many recipes are quick and easy to prepare so that a simple dinner can be on the table in less than 45 minutes from start to finish. Others are what we call fiesta dishes, more elaborate and time consuming, often served for special occasions and gatherings. Fiesta fare may require a couple of hours preparation or, at the very least, a helping hand in the kitchen. But as is often the case with ethnic cooking, preparation and organization are the keys to success. I find that planning ahead and breaking down long recipes into several small ones make the job much less formidable.

I will admit, though, that by embarking on the Filipino culinary track you are definitely taking the road less traveled. And although many of the ingredients essential to these recipes are now available in larger grocery stores, preparing for these recipes may require a trip to an Asian market. If you've never ventured into one, the unfamiliar sights and smells may be unnerving, perhaps even intimidating. But don't be overwhelmed by the twelve different varieties of soy sauce or the multiple aisles dedicated solely to noodles. My best advice to those of you new to Filipino cuisine is to accept and enjoy your status as a novice. Discovery is an exciting component of cooking that we often forgo en route to quick, convenient meals.

At the end of this book you'll find a guide to buying Filipino ingredients, a resource that details uncommon ingredients needed for the recipes so that you can navigate through the aisles with knowledge and confidence. It includes a Mail-Order and Online Shopping Guide to help you browse the virtual Asian grocer if a brick and mortar market isn't close by. It is a wonderful source for noodles, pastes, spices, condiments, sauces, and other hard-to-find ingredients. You'll find a wide selection of dry, canned, or bottled goods along with cookware, cookbooks, and recipes. Two sites in particular, templeofthai.com and importfood.com, even offer a short selection of fresh produce, which they sell individually or together in a kit. Once you've assembled your Filipino pantry, be assured that with practice and frequency you will become comfortable with what was once foreign to you inspiring you toward further culinary adventures.

THE BASICS

How do you prepare yourself and your kitchen for a Filipino meal? Naturally, you start with the building blocks: the sauces, stocks, and flavor bases that form the backbone of a cuisine. A good-quality stock is the foundation for soups and stews and can easily be the difference between creating either mediocre or memorable food. Seafood stocks are not only the quickest and easiest to prepare but, in my opinion, the most worthwhile since flavorful fish or shrimp stock is hard to find at your run-of-the-mill-grocery store. Chicken stock will require a couple of dedicated hours simmering on the stove and beef stock four to six hours, which is why the time invested into a homemade stock is certainly a persuasive factor in resorting to canned broth or bouillon. However, their inferior quality will become apparent when you try reducing your stock into a rich, bodacious sauce and the resulting liquid is flimsy and unremarkable. Good-quality stock is relatively simple to prepare and a powerful tool to add body, complexity, color, and flavor to any dish in any cuisine.

There are definitive flavors that either individually or in combination characterize Filipino cuisine. *Adobo*, a Spanish import from Mexico, is one of the culinary cornerstones that give Filipino food its flavor identity. Despite sharing a similar name, New World adobo is completely different in its anatomy than the island version, where adobo is as much a cooking technique as it is a specific dish. Literally translated, it means "preserved" or "marinated" in Spanish. In the Filipino kitchen, it refers to food cooked with five specific ingredients: vinegar, soy sauce, bay leaves, garlic, and peppercorns. This flavor formula is quintessentially Filipino and can be applied to any type of meat, seafood, or vegetable. Of course, there are variations on adobo that include the addition of coconut milk, ginger, tomato, or pineapple. But underneath the seasonings are the same five ingredients that support adobo's recognizable flavors. Because adobo is considered a national dish of the Philippines eaten in some variation all across the islands, I wanted to address its importance here even though the adobo recipes are in later chapters.

Sofrito is another flavor base imported by the Spaniards that Filipinos integrated into everyday meals. Garlic, onion, and tomato sautéed together in oil is the triumvirate that underlies *guisados* (sautés), stews, and stir-fries. Sofrito may include bell peppers for sweetness or *atsuete* (annatto) seeds for color, which like adobo, can vary depending on which cook you ask.

Toasted garlic is on equal footing with soy sauce and pepper when it comes to seasoning Filipino food. Garlic is an essential ingredient cooked with tomatoes or onions in a sofrito base. But the flavor difference of garlic when fried to a crispy golden brown and sprinkled on top *sinangag*, fried rice with garlic, or *arroz caldo*, chicken and rice soup, is a subtle addition that lingers on the tongue and elevates the ordinary to a sophisticated plane. Once you've toasted your garlic, don't feel as if you have to store it away until you plan your next Filipino meal. Add a dash to your container of sea salt or lightly crush it as a substitute for garlic powder in spice rubs or marinades.

A Filipino meal is hardly complete without an array of potent and vibrant dipping sauces (*sawsawan*), which add zest and balance to each bite. From bottled banana ketchup to sinus-clearing shrimp paste, there is always at least one sawsawan on the table to spoon over rice, to dip grilled meats or fish, or to mix into soups. A saucer filled with *toyomansi* is a common complement; it is a light mixture of soy sauce and calamansi (native lime) juice that is so popular it's been bottled and made commercially available. Fish sauce and native vinegar is another classic combination that is easily transformed by substituting soy sauce or by adding garlic and fresh herbs. Although commercial sweet chili sauces are aplenty at the Asian store, the recipe included in this chapter rivals any store-bought brand and is a cinch to put together with ingredients you're likely to already have in your pantry. A recipe for plain steamed rice, a basic component in nearly every Filipino meal, is also included in this chapter.

Fish Stock

Seafood stocks are relatively simple to prepare and a wonderful asset to add extra punch to any seafood dish from chowder to paella to stews. It is best to use fish bones or heads from nonoily fish such as flounder, sole, or snapper to produce a clean-tasting stock. Bones from oily fish such as salmon or mackerel produce an oily overpowering stock.

Makes 6 cups (1½ liters)

1 to 1½ lbs (450 to 675 g) fish
  bones
1 carrot, sliced into 1-in (2½-cm)
  pieces
2 stalks celery, sliced into 1-in
  (2½-cm) pieces
1 bay leaf
5 to 6 green onions (scallions)
2 cloves garlic, peeled
One ½-in (1½-cm) cube fresh ginger,
  peeled
5 to 7 cups (1 to 1½ liters) water

Spread all of the ingredients evenly on a sheet pan. Place the pan under the broiler 6 to 8 inches (15 to 20 cm) from the flame for 12 to 15 minutes. Periodically turn the bones and vegetables to brown all the sides. Place the roasted vegetables and fish bones in a medium stockpot (3 to 4 quarts/liters). Pour in water to cover the ingredients by 1 inch (2½ cm). Bring the stock to a boil, then reduce the heat to a simmer for 45 minutes to 1 hour. Strain the stock through a fine sieve. Discard vegetables and bones. Cool stock. Store in the refrigerator for up to 1 week or in the freezer for 3 months.

Variation: Shrimp Stock. Substitute the fish bones with shrimp shells from 2 pounds (900 g) raw shrimp for the fish bones.

Beef Stock

Choose meaty beef bones from the neck, knuckles, ribs, or shank to produce a rich, flavorful beef stock. I particularly like supplementing my beef bones with a few cuts of oxtail, which are packed with collagen and produce an incomparably thick gelatinous broth. Oxtail used to be a throwaway cut, the scraps that were left to the dog. However, its revival on upscale restaurant menus has elevated the demand and the price so that it is no longer a true bargain. Using oxtail for stock reaps double rewards—a bosomy broth and the simmered oxtail meat, tender and supercharged with flavor that begs to be added to soups, stews, or pastas.

Makes 4 to 5 quarts (3¾ to 4¾ liters)

4 lbs (1¾ kg) beef bones plus
  1 lb (450 g) cut oxtail
2 large onions, quartered
5 green onions (scallions), whole
3 large carrots, cut into 1-in (2½-cm)
  pieces
4 celery stalks, cut into 1-in (2½-cm)
  pieces
4 to 5 cloves garlic, peeled
1 cup (250 ml) rice wine
2 bay leaves
5 to 6 quarts (4¾ to 5 liters) water

Brown the bones: Preheat the oven to 400°F (200°C). Place the bones, onions, green onions (scallions), carrots, celery, and garlic in a large roasting pan. Roast the bones and vegetables in the oven 1 to 1½ hours, occasionally turning the bones and vegetables so that they are browned on all sides but not burnt. Remove the roasting pan from the oven and quickly transfer the bones and vegetables to a large pot. While the roasting pan is still hot, deglaze the roasting pan with the rice wine, scraping any toasted bits of meat or vegetables from the pan. Pour the wine and scrapings into the pot with the bones and vegetables. Add the bay leaves and water. There should be enough water so that there is at least 2 to 3 inches (5 to 8 cm) of water covering the bones.

Simmer the stock: Bring the stock to a boil. Using a ladle, skim and discard the foam that rises to the top. Reduce the heat to a simmer and cook the stock 4 to 5 hours. Remove the meaty bones and oxtail and set aside on a plate. Strain the stock through a fine sieve into a large container. Discard the vegetables and aromatic herbs. Cool the stock and bones to room temperature. Skim off the fat from the surface of the stock or refrigerate the stock and scrape off the hardened fat. Use your fingers to pull the meat off the bones. Discard the bones and gristle. Reserve the meat for another use. Store the broth in the refrigerator for up to 1 week or freeze in ice cube trays or small containers for up to 3 months.

Chicken Stock and Flaked Chicken

Whether you're whipping up a warm soup, braising a roast, or cooking rice pilaf, a light and versatile chicken stock is an invaluable ingredient that adds flavor and depth to your food. Here is a simple recipe for a light chicken stock that calls for simmering a whole chicken so that you are left not only with the broth but with tender cooked chicken that can be used in countless recipes for your favorite salads, casseroles, or soups. The broth can be frozen in ice cube trays or small containers for convenient use. Portion the chicken into ½ to 1 pound (225 to 450 g) bags that can be defrosted quickly.

Yields 8 to 10 cups (1¾ to 2¼ liters) stock and 1 lb (450 g) cooked chicken

4 to 5 lbs (2 to 2½ kg) whole chicken
2 medium onions, diced
2 stalks celery, chopped into 2-in (5-cm) pieces
2 large carrots, peeled and chopped into 2-in (5-cm) pieces
4 cloves garlic, peeled
1 bay leaf
One ½-in (1-cm) cube fresh ginger, peeled
6 black peppercorns
10 to 12 cups (2¼ to 3 liters) cold water

Prepare the chicken: Remove the giblets packet from the cavity of the chicken. Reserve the neck bone for the stock. Rinse the inside and outside of the chicken thoroughly under cold water.

Make the stock: Place the chicken and neck bone in a large stockpot (6 quarts/liters) with the remaining ingredients. There should be enough water in the pot so that there is at least 1 inch (3 cm) of water covering the chicken. Over a high flame, bring the water to a boil. Using a ladle, skim and discard any foam that rises to the top of the stock. Reduce the stock to a simmer over medium heat for 2 to 2½ hours.

Strain the stock and flake the chicken: Cool the stock to room temperature. Remove the chicken from the pot. Pour the stock through a fine sieve into a large container. Discard the vegetables, bay leaf, ginger, and peppercorns. Use a ladle to skim the fat off the broth or refrigerate the broth and scrape off the solidified fat. The chicken will be very tender and easy to pull from the bones using your hands. Flake the chicken into small chunks, discarding any skin, bones, or cartilage. Store the broth in the refrigerator for up to 1 week or freeze for up to 3 months. The chicken may be refrigerated for 4 days or frozen for up to 3 months.

Vegetable Stock

Vegetable stock, with its light, neutral taste, is a versatile ingredient that can be used in practically any dish to add both moisture and flavor. Not only does vegetable stock take little time to make, but it is easily assembled with ingredients you probably already have in your refrigerator. It's also an economic way to utilize wilted vegetables that are past their prime.

Makes 4 cups (1 liter)

½ lb (225 g) onions, quartered
½ lb (225 g) carrots, peeled and cut into thirds
¼ lb (125 g) celery stalks, cut in into thirds
2 whole green onions (scallions), cut in half
4 cloves garlic, peeled
One ¼-in (6-mm)-slice peeled fresh ginger
6 to 7 black peppercorns
1 bay leaf
5 cups (1¼ liters) water

Place all ingredients in a 2 to 3-quart/liter pot. Bring stock to a boil and skim off foam that rises to the surface. Lower heat to a simmer and cook for 1½ hours. Strain stock through a fine sieve and discard vegetables. Cool stock to room temperature. Store in the refrigerator for up to two weeks or freeze for up to 6 months.

Coconut Cream Latik

The Philippines is one of the world's largest producers of coconuts, which explains why Filipino cuisine would only narrowly exist without the fundamental flavors and textures lent by the myriad of edibles from the coconut palm. Notwithstanding the tender palm hearts and the valuable sap used for sugar cakes, syrup, alcoholic beverages, and vinegar, the coconut fruit itself is the source of precious coconut water, meat, oil, and milk. I remember making coconut milk the old-fashioned way: sitting on a short rectangular bench to which my grandfather attached a serrated metal blade used to finely grate the flesh of mature coconuts. We'd steep the grated meat in the water collected from the center of the nut and squeeze the pulp to extract thick coconut cream. A second steeping of the pulp with tap water extracted thin coconut milk. A traditional recipe for *latik* starts off by slowly cooking the first press of thick coconut cream until the coconut solids caramelize and the coconut oil separates and rises to the top. However, I know that there aren't too many people grating coconuts in their spare time to make coconut cream. In this recipe canned or frozen coconut milk is the convenient base that's easily simmered to evaporate water, leaving you with a smooth creamy latik. Look for the Chaokoh brand of canned coconut milk, my preferred choice, which has a considerable amount of thick coconut cream.

Makes ½ cup (125 ml)
1 (13-oz/400-ml) can coconut milk

Pour the coconut milk into a small saucepan and simmer over low-medium heat for 40 to 45 minutes. Cool the reduced coconut cream to room temperature and refrigerate. Once chilled, it will have the consistency of cream cheese. Store in an airtight container in the refrigerator for up to 2 weeks.

The longer you cook the coconut milk, the darker and thicker it will become. As the coconut milk reduces, the coconut solids will begin to caramelize and the coconut oil will rise to the surface. Whisk the mixture occasionally during cooking to reincorporate the oil and smooth out the mixture. If you find that you've overreduced the coconut milk and that it is too thick (perhaps you need it to be spreadable or pourable), simply add water to thin it to your desired consistency.

Sautéed Shrimp Paste
Guisadong Bagoong Hipon

Bagoong, pronounced "bah-GOO-ong," is neither easy on the nose nor on the eyes. But this fermented seafood paste, though pungent, perhaps even offensive to some, is a signature ingredient in Southeast Asia that adds dimension and complexity to the food. Bagoong is available jarred in the condiments section of the Asian market and can be purchased in different fish and shrimp varieties, the most common being *bagoong hipon* (also called shrimp fry), *bagoong teron* (bonnet mouth fish), *bagoong padas* (siganid fish), and *bagoong monamon* (anchovies and scad). Bagoong is added to soups, stir-fries, and stews not only as a salt alternative but also for its unique flavor. If served alongside a dish as a condiment, it can be served straight from the jar, although it's typically sautéed with a sofrito of garlic, scallion, and tomato before being brought to the table.

Makes 3 tablespoons
1 tablespoon olive oil
1 tablespoon finely chopped green onions (scallions), white parts only
1 small clove garlic, minced
2 tablespoons diced tomato
1 tablespoon shrimp paste
Dash of freshly ground black pepper

Heat the olive oil in a small skillet over medium heat. When the oil is hot but not smoking, add the green onions (scallions), garlic, and tomato. Cook and stir for 1 to 2 minutes until the vegetables soften. Add the shrimp paste and cook for another minute until heated through. Season with pepper. Serve in a small bowl.

Serving suggestions: Odd as it may seem, bagoong is a classic condiment paired with sour green mangoes, although I equally enjoy it with sweet ripe mangoes. Filipinos are hugely keen on the salty-sour or salty-sweet flavor dynamic that makes this dish a popular snack. Dab a little bagoong on boiled or fried plantain bananas. Add a small dollop to your pickled dishes such as Achara (page 62). Straying from Filipino cuisine, bagoong monamon (anchovies and scad) is very versatile and works wonderfully in dressings for Caesar salad, Niçoise salad, and potato salad. Mix bagoong monamon with softened butter or cream cheese, spices, and herbs for a quick cracker spread. A dash of bagoong monamon with sherry, mustard, lemon, and parsley makes a great pan sauce for steak.

Curry-Tomato Sofrito

This unique, curry-flavored *sofrito* works double duty as both a flavor base and a sauce. The tomatoes are slowly baked in the oven with garlic, curry, and plenty of olive oil. The result is a rich tomato sauce instead of the classic sofrito paste.

What I love about this sofrito is its easy versatility paired with noodles, ladled on grilled chicken, or even topped on fish such as Milkfish with Pili Nut Stuffing (page 124). For a quick noodle dish, heat the sofrito with fresh basil or mint and toss with pasta. For a quick seafood dinner, heat the sofrito with a little seafood stock and add clams or mussels to the pan. Cover and steam until the shells open and serve with lemon and crusty bread.

Makes 3 cups (750 ml)
2 pints (575 g) cherry tomatoes, stems removed
2 cloves garlic, minced
1 green onion (scallion), finely chopped

¼ teaspoon minced fresh ginger
1 tablespoon soy sauce
1 tablespoon yellow curry paste or curry powder
½ cup (125 ml) olive oil
¼ teaspoon ground black pepper

Preheat the oven to 325°F (160°C). Place all the ingredients in a medium baking dish and cover with aluminum foil. Bake for 1 hour until the tomatoes have completely collapsed and released all of their juices. Cool to room temperature. Store in an airtight container in the refrigerator for up to 1 week or freeze for up to 3 months.

Edam Butter

Makes ⅔ cup (75 g)
2 oz (50 g) unsalted butter, at room temperature
¼ cup (25 g) finely grated Edam cheese (substitute gouda)
1 tablespoon finely grated Parmesan cheese
1 tablespoon honey
¼ teaspoon salt
Dash of freshly ground black pepper

Combine the butter, Edam, Parmesan, honey, salt, and pepper in a bowl. Mix until well combined. Spoon the butter into a ramekin or small bowl. Serve at room temperature with Suman Nga Baboy, or Steamed Rice Cakes (page 28). Store in an airtight container in the refrigerator for up to 3 weeks.

Toasted Garlic and Garlic Oil

In Filipino cuisine, there's no such thing as a little garlic. Present in our *sofrito*, marinades, and dipping sauces, raw, roasted, or sautéed, garlic is one of the essential answers to flavorful food.

Transformed by a little oil and heat, toasted garlic is commonly sprinkled on dishes as a finishing condiment to add an extra boost of flavor. Filipinos often serve toasted garlic as a topping for rice porridge (page 50), or fried rice (page 79), but I find it a versatile ingredient sprinkled on top of casseroles, soups, salads, even mixed into my spice rubs for chicken or pork.

Makes approximately ¼ cup (15 g) toasted garlic and 1 cup (250 ml) garlic oil
1 teaspoon sesame oil
1 cup (250 ml) olive oil or vegetable oil
8 to 10 cloves garlic, chopped
Pinch of salt

Heat the oils in a small skillet and warm over low to medium heat. Add the chopped garlic. Cook and stir the garlic until it has lightly browned, 4 to 6 minutes. Pour the garlic and oil through a fine sieve over a bowl, reserving the garlic oil. Dry the garlic on paper towels. Cool the garlic and infused oil. Store separately in an airtight container for up to 3 months.

Five-Spice Vinegar

Filipinos are addicted to the amazing versatility and indelible zing of vinegar. Not just reserved for pickling or preserving, vinegar is an essential flavor component in dishes ranging from marinated *kilaw* (raw fish, similar to seviche) to slowly stewed *adobo* (a national Filipino dish) to refreshing *sinigang,* hot and sour soup. For an all-purpose vinegar, I prefer the native coconut or palm vinegar that is readily available in Asian markets and to my surprise even carried in select chain grocery stores. Coconut and nipa vinegars are mildly acidic and leave a clean finish with just a hint of sweetness. Most important, they do not overpower the food, allowing the ingredients of your dish to shine.

This recipe infuses vinegar with the bold flavors of five-spice to add a wonderful dimension to certain dishes such as the Scallop Kilaw (page 64), Salmon Kilaw (page 73) and pickled vegetable Achara (page 62). Using a combination of the five individual spices over five-spice powder will allow you to control the infusion of delicate flavors while keeping the color and texture of the vinegar intact. If at all possible avoid five-spice powder for this recipe. I go through a lot of this vinegar, so I add my spices directly to my bottle of vinegar. For smaller batches, simply use a glass jar to hold the vinegar and spices. Once all the vinegar is used, add more without replacing the spices. The spices will impart their flavors through 2 to 3 steepings.

Makes 2 cups (500 ml)
2 cups (500 ml) coconut or palm vinegar
2 pieces star anise
1 bay leaf
1 cinnamon stick
1 teaspoon whole black peppercorns
1 teaspoon fennel seeds
5 cloves

Place all the ingredients together in a glass jar and allow the spices to impart their flavor for at least 24 hours before using. Store the jar in a cool dry place for up to 6 months.

Basic Dipping Sauces Sawsawan

A Filipino table is incomplete without the littering of small dishes filled with *sawsawan,* dipping sauces, to add the piquant heat of chiles, the puckery tang of citrus, or the heady zest of shrimp paste to the food as each person prefers. All-purpose dipping combinations such as vinegar and soy sauce, garlic and fish sauce, or *calamansi* and chilies are served to enliven simply prepared foods such as grilled fish or broiled chicken. More elaborate sawsawan such as the liver sauce served with spit-roasted suckling pig *(lechon)* or the garlicky sweet and sour sauce served with fresh spring rolls *(lumpia sariwa)* are reserved for specific dishes. I've included here just a few easy and basic dipping sauces that intensify the flavors of grilled or roasted meats, poultry, fish, and vegetables. Experiment with different herbs to add an extra layer of high impact flavor to your dipping sauces.

Toyomansi: makes 1⅔ tablespoons
1 tablespoon soy sauce
2 teaspoons calamansi juice

Spicy Garlic: makes 3 tablespoons
2 tablespoons coconut or palm vinegar
1 small Thai chile, chopped
1 clove garlic, minced

Green Ginger: makes 2⅔ tablespoons
2 tablespoons calamansi juice
1 teaspoon chopped fresh coriander leaves (cilantro)
1 teaspoon minced ginger

Shrimp Paste: makes 2⅓ tablespoons
2 tablespoons coconut or palm vinegar
1 teaspoon shrimp paste *(bagoong hipon)*

Sweet and Sour: Makes 2⅔ tablespoons
1 tablespoon soy sauce
1 tablespoon mirin
2 teaspoons calamansi juice

Sweet Chili Sauce: makes ½ cup (125 ml)
½ cup (125 ml) corn syrup
2 cloves garlic, minced
1 tablespoon coconut or palm vinegar
2 teaspoons chili flakes or sambal ulek
½ teaspoon minced ginger

Combine in a saucepan. Simmer for 5 minutes to marry the flavors. Cool to room temperature before serving.

Lumpia Sariwa Dipping Sauce

Makes ½ cup (125 ml)
1 tablespoon olive oil
1 clove garlic, minced
2 teaspoons all-purpose flour
½ cup (125 ml) water
2 tablespoons soy sauce
1 tablespoon brown sugar
2 teaspoons vinegar
¼ cup (25 g) finely chopped
    roasted peanuts or cashews

Heat the olive oil in a small saucepan over medium heat. When the pan is hot add the garlic. Cook and stir the garlic for 30 seconds until golden brown. Stir in the flour and mix with the garlic and oil to form a paste. Add the water, soy sauce, brown sugar, and vinegar. Use a whisk to dissolve the liquids with the flour paste. Simmer for 3 to 4 minutes until thick, constantly whisking until smooth. Cool the sauce and pour into a serving dish. Sprinkle the sauce with the chopped nuts and serve with lumpia sariwa (page 40).

Mushroom Soy Dipping Sauce

Makes 3 tablespoons
2 tablespoons mushroom soy
    sauce
1½ teaspoons palm or coconut
    vinegar
1 clove roasted garlic, mashed
1 teaspoon mirin
¼ teaspoon salt
Dash of freshly ground black
    pepper

Combine the soy sauce, vinegar, mashed garlic, and mirin in a medium bowl. Season with salt and pepper. Pour into a dipping sauce bowl and serve alongside Suman Nga Baboy, or Steamed Rice Cakes (page 28).

Eggplant-Prune Compote

Makes approximately 4 cups (600 g)
Serves 4 as a side dish
1 tablespoon butter
1 small onion, sliced
2 cloves garlic, chopped
¼ cup (50 ml) coconut or palm vinegar
2 tablespoons soy sauce
¼ teaspoon ground black pepper
1 cup (250 ml) Chicken Stock (see
    page 15)
1 small eggplant, cut into 1-in
    (2½-cm) cubes
1 cup (150 g) chopped prunes
¼ cup (25 g) toasted and chopped
    pili nuts (substitute pine nuts)

Melt the butter in a medium sauté pan over medium-high heat. Add the sliced onion and cook until browned and caramelized, stirring occasionally, 6 to 8 minutes. Add the garlic and cook for another 2 to 3 minutes. Deglaze the pan with the vinegar, scraping any browned bits of onion off the bottom of the pan. Add the soy sauce, pepper, chicken stock, eggplant, and prunes. Reduce the heat to a simmer and cook until the eggplant is tender, 8 to 10 minutes. Stir in the pili nuts and spoon alongside the grilled grouper (page 129).

This naturally sweet compote also pairs well with Whole Roasted Red Snapper (page 125), Bistek (page 112), Oven Roasted Pork (page 107), and Stuffed Quail (page 103).

Tomato, Onion, and Garlic Paste
Basic Sofrito

Sofrito is originally a Spanish paste of cooked tomato, onion, bell pepper, and garlic used as a flavor base for any number of soups, stews, and sautés. Naturally, the different Spanish colonies have long since indi-vidualized their sofrito so that in Puerto Rico it is different from the sofrito of Cuba or Mexico. In the Philippines, we start many of our dishes with a basic trio of onion, gar-lic, and tomato sautéed in olive oil. Depending on the dish being made, *atsuete* (annatto) seeds may be add-ed to impart a burnt russet color and earthy flavor to the oil before adding the garlic, onion, and tomato. Other times, bell peppers are added for sweetness. You can certainly tailor your sofrito to suit your own taste. This recipe gives you a basic flavor template that you can build upon with other ingredients. Keeping a sofrito reserve in your refrigerator will allow you to save time chop-ping onions, garlic, and tomatoes.

Makes 2 cups (450 g)
3 tablespoons olive oil
1 large yellow onion, diced
4 cloves garlic, chopped
2 large tomatoes, diced
1 tablespoon soy sauce
½ teaspoon freshly ground black
    pepper

Heat the olive oil in a small sauté pan (1 to 2 quarts/liters) over medium heat. When the oil is hot but not smoking, add the onion. Cook and stir for 3 to 4 minutes until translucent. Add the garlic and cook for another minute. Add the tomatoes and cook for 5 to 7 minutes, until tomatoes completely collapse and all the liquid from the to-matoes has evaporated. Season with soy sauce and pepper. Remove from the heat and cool. Store in an airtight container in the refrigerator for up to 1 week.

Variations: 1. With annatto seeds.
To add a light earthy flavor and russet color to your sofrito, first sauté 2 teaspoons *atsuete* (annatto) seeds in olive oil for 4 to 5 minutes. Remove the seeds from the oil, which should have an orange color. Discard the seeds and continue directions for basic sofrito.

2. With bell peppers. Green bell peppers will add a grassy flavor and red bell peppers will impart their characteristic sweetness. Use one small bell pepper, deseeded and chopped into a fine dice. Follow the original recipe sautéing the pepper with the onion.

3. With misu. Misu sofrito, or sofrito with miso paste, is especially delicious as a base for seafood soups and sautés. You'll see it used in the Pesa nga may Misu (page 126) although it also pairs well with poultry. In this recipe, I find that caramelizing the onions in butter creates a nice sweetness that is surprisingly delicious paired against the salty miso. See Misu in "Buying Filipino Ingredients," (see page 171).

Melt 1 tablespoon butter in a large sauté pan over medium-high heat. Add 1 thinly sliced yellow onion, approximately 1 cup (80 g). Stir and cook for 8 to 10 minutes until browned and well caramelized. Add 1 minced garlic clove and 1 small diced tomato. Sauté for 5 to 7 minutes until the tomato softens. Stir in ½ cup (125 g) miso paste and stir to combine. Cook another 2 to 3 minutes. Cool and store in an airtight container in the refrigerator for up to 2 weeks. Yields 1 cup (250 g).

The thread that weaves through nearly every Filipino table from Luzon to Mindanao is the humble grain of rice. Whether served as the most important component of a meal or as the basis of a quick snack—as shown here in Fragrant Rice with Green Mango (recipe, page 79)—rice is what Filipinos equate with sustenance. Without flair or flourish, steamed white rice is ideal. Long-grain *indica* varieties are the most widely grown on the islands, which include the jasminelike *milagrosa* variety that is so popular for its floral aroma and fresh-cooked stickiness. Many Filipinos rely on their electric rice cookers to steam rice to fluffy perfection, but equal results can be achieved on the stovetop.

Serves 6
3 cups (600 g) long-
    grain rice
5 cups water

Place your rice in a large deep pot. Wash the rice thoroughly in several changes of water until the water runs clear. This washing will give your rice a cleaner flavor and whiteness. Drain all of the water from the rice.

Pour 5 cups water into the rice pot. Cover the pot and place over high heat. Bring the water to a boil. This may take 5 to 7 minutes. Turn the heat to the lowest heat setting and allow the rice to steam for 12 to 18 minutes until the rice is tender and all the liquid has been absorbed. Turn off the heat and allow the rice to continue steaming for 10 minutes before removing the cover. This method of cooking rice yields a fluffy, moist, and sticky rice. Serve hot.

Varation: Pandan Steamed Rice.
After you have washed your rice, add a 5-inch (12¾-cm) pandan leaf to the pot. Cook the rice as directed.

SHANGHAI EGG ROLLS LUMPIA SHANGHAI

PORK AND GINGER DUMPLINGS SHUMAI

STEAMED RICE CAKES WITH BACON AND CARAMELIZED ONIONS SUMAN NGA BABOY

SHRIMP AND SWEET POTATO FRITTERS UKOY

CHICKEN LIVER MOUSSE

ADOBO-FLAVORED PECANS

BEEF TURNOVERS EMPANADAS

FRIED SWEET BANANAS PRITONG SAGING

GRILLED CHICKEN WINGS

STEAMED BUNS FILLED WITH CURRY CHICKEN CURRY CHICKEN SIOPAO

CRÊPES WITH SHRIMP AND GREEN PAPAYA LUMPIA SARIWA

SPICED ANCHOVY CRISPS PRITONG DILIS

APPETIZERS AND SMALL BITES

Pampagana may be the Filipino word for appetizer, but *merienda* (snack), *pulutan* (bar food), or *pica-pica* (finger food) suggest the same qualities of an appetizer—such as their small size and ability to kick-start the appetite. However, an appetizer implies a meal served in courses, a Western custom that Filipinos don't typically follow. Filipinos instead place equal importance on every dish so that all offerings, from salad to soup to the main dish, are brought to the table at the same time. Despite the lack of an appetizer course, per se, Filipinos still embrace every occasion to partake in small dishes, appetite teasers, and grazing tidbits of finger food enjoyed with a beer or glass of wine. The focus of this chapter is on recipes that in the American tradition make good appetizers, casually passed or shared in a large group during the cocktail hour or served individually in a more formal setting.

If you have ever experienced the excitement of Chinese dim sum with the traffic jam of carts wheeling towers of ministeamers to your table, presenting everything from chicken feet to dumplings to silken tofu, you'll recognize several of the dishes in this chapter. Although not originally Filipino cuisine, centuries of trade with China have deposited dim sum on the islands as an adopted presence, similar to the way pizza has become a transplanted American staple. You'll see Shumai pork dumplings, best served piping hot directly from the steamer; lumpia egg rolls in different incarnations, from crispy, fried Lumpia Shanghai to the tender and elegant Lumpia Sariwa; and Siopao, steamed buns filled with curry chicken, although the possibilities of fillings are deliciously endless.

One homeland tradition supplanted by the ubiquitous busy schedule is the taking of merienda, the midmorning and midafternoon refreshment that Filipinos enjoy in between main meals. I often think of merienda fare in terms of what my parents would serve to their friends during a lazy, Sunday afternoon mahjong game. Literally translated from Spanish as "snack," merienda can be sweet or savory, light or heavy, and may include something as modest as Saging, fried bananas sprinkled with sugar, or a more filling snack of Empanadas, hand-held meat pies. One item that merienda will typically not include is steamed white rice, which presumes serving a heavy meal that would interfere with the anticipation of lunch or dinner. However, I have included in this chapter one of my favorite rice snacks, Suman, small pouches of sticky rice steamed in banana leaves that are eaten as a snack instead of the anchor of a meal.

Filipinos, like much of the world, appreciate their drink. And just as rice is essential in a Filipino meal, pulutan, or finger food, is crucial to the enjoyment of a cold bottle of San Miguel beer, *tuba* coconut wine, or Tanduay rum. Pulutan is the Filipino equivalent of "bar food" and can vary in range from simple snacks featured in this chapter, such as Adobo-Flavored Pecans, spicy Spiced Anchovy Crisps, or Grilled Chicken Wings, to more elaborate stir-fried dishes like *sigsig*, a native delicacy of stir-fried crispy pig skin with onions and chiles, or even the exotic snake, turtle, or monitor lizard pulutan desired for its supposed aphrodisiac qualities. Whatever the pulutan may be, the point is that it's best served with a potent beverage equally suited for toasting the joys of life and clearing the throat for the second (or third) round.

SHANGHAI EGG ROLLS LUMPIA SHANGHAI

These egg rolls are unique for a few reasons. The pencil-thin rolls have an elegant striking appearance very different from the thick stuffed egg rolls typically seen at the local Chinese takeout restaurant. They are primarily filled with a thin line of seasoned pork and wrapped with a special *lumpia* wrapper, which once cooked, has a perfectly smooth surface and an extra crispy crunch.

Makes 30 8-in/20-cm lumpia

1 lb (450 g) lean ground pork
1 clove garlic, minced
1½ teaspoons peeled and minced
   fresh ginger
2 tablespoons oyster sauce
1 tablespoon soy sauce
Dash of freshly ground black
   pepper
½ cup (50 g) finely shredded
   Napa cabbage
1 package (11 oz/310 g/25
   sheets) lumpia wrappers (substitute frozen Chinese-style
   spring roll wrappers or
   Vietnamese rice paper wrappers)
1 large egg, beaten

Make the filling: Combine the pork, garlic, ginger, oyster sauce, soy sauce, and pepper in a large bowl and mix very well so that the seasonings are evenly distributed throughout the meat. Add the cabbage and mix again to evenly distribute through the meat. Set aside in the refrigerator until ready to use.

Prepare the wrappers: Using a sharp serrated knife, cut the square of wrappers in half through the center so that you have two stacks of rectangular wrappers. Gently pull apart each wrapper. They are much easier to separate once they have been cut into smaller sheets. Once separated, keep the wrappers stacked together and covered with a towel or in a plastic freezer bag so that they do not become dry.

Form the egg rolls: Place one rectangular wrapper horizontally on your workspace with the long edge facing you. Take a tablespoon of filling and, using your fingers, form it into a thin continuous line about ½ inch (1 cm) above the wrapper's bottom edge. Lightly moisten your fingertips with water to prevent the meat from sticking to them. Pull the wrapper's bottom edge over the filling and roll it up like a cigarette. Brush the top edge with the beaten egg to seal the egg roll. Lay the egg roll seam side down on a cookie sheet or tray lined with parchment or wax paper. Continue rolling egg rolls with the remaining meat and wrappers.

Once you've filled the tray, place a sheet of parchment or wax paper on the first layer of egg rolls and place a second layer on top. Do not stack more than two layers on one tray. The weight of a third layer will flatten the first. To freeze lumpia, cover your tray of egg rolls with plastic wrap and place the entire tray in the freezer for 2 to 3 hours until firm. Once firm, remove from the tray and store in freezer bags for up to 3 months.

Cook the egg rolls: Fry in 350°F (175°C) oil for 3 to 5 minutes, until golden brown on all sides. Drain on paper towels and cut in half to form 4-inch (10-cm) pieces. If lumpia are frozen, fry 5 to 7 minutes until golden brown on all sides and the meat filling is cooked through.

These crunchy egg rolls are best served immediately while hot. It is possible to fry lumpia 2 to 3 hours ahead of time and still serve them hot and crisp at a gathering. Place previously fried egg rolls in a single layer on a baking sheet. Place in a preheated 250°F (120°C) oven for 25 minutes to recrisp the wrappers before serving. Serve immediately with commercially-prepared or homemade sweet chili sauce (page 18).

PORK AND GINGER DUMPLINGS SHUMAI

Two of my loyal Rambutan customers, Jennifer and Langdon Vaningen, lovingly coined these open-faced dumplings "Oh my! Shumai," which instantly became the restaurant's unofficial name for these bite-sized gems packed with a mouthful of flavor. I use the same meat filling in my Lumpia Shanghai (page 24)—long, cigar-thin egg rolls that, despite sharing a common filling, taste very different due to their being fried instead of steamed. Be patient with the dumpling-making process, which can be frustrating at first. Once the learning curve kicks in, usually by the fifth or sixth dumpling, you'll be making them with impressive speed. Although these dumplings are served more as an appetizer or midday snack, the simple addition of rice and a vegetable turn *shumai* into a complete and satisfying meal.

Makes 30 dumplings

1 lb (450 g) lean ground pork
1 clove garlic, minced
1½ teaspoons peeled and minced
    fresh ginger
2 tablespoons oyster sauce
1 tablespoon soy sauce
Pinch of freshly ground black
    pepper
½ cup (50 g) finely shredded Napa
    cabbage
1 package (50 pieces) round
    dumpling wrappers

Make the filling: Combine the pork, garlic, ginger, oyster sauce, soy sauce, and pepper in a large bowl and mix very well so that the seasonings are evenly distributed throughout the meat. Add the cabbage and mix again to evenly distribute through the meat.

Form the dumplings: Start by very lightly moistening the edges of a dumpling wrapper using a pastry brush and water. Turn the wrapper over and on the dry side spread 1 heaping teaspoon of pork filling evenly toward the edge using the back of your spoon.

If you are right-handed, place the tips of your left thumb and forefinger together to form a circle. Use your right hand if left-handed. Center the dumpling wrapper, meat side up, on top of your fingers so that the center of the wrapper is in the circle of your fingers. With your spoon, gently push the center of the wrapper into the circle of your fingers while tightening your fingers around the dumpling to give it its tulip shape, leaving the top of the dumpling open. Take a little more filling and pack it in the top to give it more shape if necessary and smooth the meat.

Place the dumpling on a tray lined with parchment or wax paper. Continue with the remaining dumplings. It is important that the dumplings are not touching each other on the tray; they will stick together.

Cook the dumplings: Place the formed dumplings in a steamer. Steam for 8 to 12 minutes until the dumplings are firm when gently squeezed with tongs. Serve immediately with the dipping sauce.

DIPPING SAUCE

2 tablespoons soy sauce
1 teaspoon mashed roasted garlic
¼ teaspoon palm or coconut vine-
    gar (substitute rice vinegar)
¼ teaspoon sambal ulek or dried red
    pepper flakes

Combine all the ingredients together in a small dish. Serve alongside the hot shumai.

STEAMED RICE CAKES WITH BACON AND CARAMELIZED ONIONS
SUMAN NGA BABOY

One of my earliest kitchen memories is of my mom regularly enlisting my sister and me (it was actually more like a forced draft) to help her roll what seemed like hundreds of sweetened, steamed rice snacks on Saturday mornings. She was famous for her *suman* and often gave it to friends and co-workers, especially around the holidays. Back then, we rolled the sticky rice like egg rolls in small sheets of aluminum foil before they went into a large steamer for an hour. Now, when I wrap suman I often use banana leaves, which impart a leafy green flavor to the rice. Suman can take on a few incarnations: sweet or savory, plainly served with sugar or dipped into hot chocolate, or heavily adorned with meat and vegetables. I have presented here one of my favorite savory suman recipes, heartily flavored with musky dried mushrooms, smoky bacon, and caramelized onions. Two nontraditional accoutrements that pair exceptionally well with this dish are sweetened Edam butter (page 17) and mushroom soy dipping sauce (page 20), something a little different than the typical dipping sauces of soy and garlic or fish sauce and vinegar.

Makes 8 suman squares
3 dried shiitake mushrooms
½ cup (125 ml) rice wine
⅔ cup (150 ml) hot Chicken Stock
   (see page 15)
3 slices bacon, diced
1 small yellow onion, diced
1 cup (200 g) uncooked glutinous
   rice
1 cup (250 ml) coconut milk
¼ teaspoon salt
¼ teaspoon freshly ground black
   pepper
1 (10-oz/280-g) package banana
   leaves, thawed

Soak the mushrooms: Combine the dried mushrooms, rice wine, and hot chicken broth in a medium bowl. Soak the mushrooms for 15 to 20 minutes until caps are tender. Remove the mushrooms and squeeze the excess liquid back into the bowl. Cut off and discard the mushroom stems. Slice the mushroom caps thinly. Set the mushrooms and soaking liquid aside.

Cook the rice: Heat a medium skillet (2 to 3 quarts/liters) over medium heat. Add the diced bacon. Cook and stir the bacon for 4 to 5 minutes until much of the fat is rendered out. Add the onion and sauté another 5 to 7 minutes until the onion begins to caramelize and turns a golden color. Add the glutinous rice and stir to coat with oil. Deglaze the pan with the mushroom soaking liquid, scraping off any browned bits from the bottom of the pan.

Add the coconut milk, sliced mushrooms, salt, and pepper. Simmer the rice for 12 to 15 minutes, stirring frequently, until the rice has absorbed all of the liquid. The rice should be very thick and sticky but still firm when you bite into it.

Form and cool the rice: Turn the rice out into a 9 by 9-inch (23 by 23-cm)-square baking dish and press it into a 2-inch (5 cm)-thick block. Molding the rice this way will allow you to cut even blocks, which makes for easy wrapping. Cool the rice completely. Use a knife to cut 8 equal-sized blocks just slightly over 2 by 2 inches (5 by 5 cm)-square.

Wrap the suman: Step 1. Prepare the banana leaves by running both sides of each leaf under hot water and wiping dry with paper towels. Lay one leaf horizontally in front of you. Starting from the bottom edge closest to you, cut the leaf into 4-inch (10 cm)-wide strips, at least 6 inches (15 cm) tall from top to bottom. Each strip will be used to wrap a single suman block so make sure you have enough strips for the number of blocks. **Step 2.** Cut an equal number of ¼-inch (½-cm) leaf strips. These thin strips will be used to tie the suman closed, like a ribbon. **Step 3.** Center 1 rice block on the bottom edge of a leaf strip. Pull the bottom edge over the rice and roll the block in the leaf like a gift. Fold in the sides and hold them secured with your fingers. Tie the ¼-inch (½-cm) leaf strip around the block so that it holds the sides and top edge closed. Tie the "ribbon" into a knot. Continue wrapping the remaining blocks of suman.

Steam the suman: Place the wrapped blocks in your steamer and steam for 50 minutes. Cool slightly before serving. Serve with Edam butter (page 17) and mushroom dipping sauce (page 20).

SHRIMP AND SWEET POTATO FRITTERS UKOY

This is what I like to consider a bare-bones *ukoy* recipe upon which other variations are built. These fritters are light and crunchy with just barely enough batter to keep the sweet potato and cassava clinging to the shrimp. Other variations may include the addition of chopped green onions (scallions), bean sprouts, or water chestnuts mixed with flour and water into a pancake batter consistency. Such modifications detract from the crunchiness of the basic recipe, but the textural softening is replaced with heightened flavor. One key procedural note is to use a slicing tool that will cut long, ½ to 1-inch (13 to 25-mm) matchsticks of sweet potato and cassava. A mandoline works beautifully to slice wiry vegetable threads that cook quickly into shoestring fries surrounding the shrimp.

Makes 10 to 12 fritters

1 small sweet potato, peeled and cut into matchsticks (approximately 1½ cups/340 g)

1 small fresh cassava, peeled and cut into matchsticks (approximately 1½ cups/400 g)

½ cup (50 g) cornstarch

2 to 3 large egg whites

10 to 12 jumbo shrimp, peeled, deveined, and butterflied with tails left on

2 to 3 cups (500 to 750 ml) oil, for frying

Make the batter: Combine the sweet potato, cassava, and cornstarch in a large bowl. Toss the vegetables to evenly coat with the cornstarch. Add the egg whites little by little and mix with the vegetables until just moistened and gluey. The vegetables should be thick and sticky when pressed together.

Form the fritters: Sandwich the body of a butterflied shrimp in between two spoonfuls of sweet potato batter and press the fritter together. The tail should be left sticking out. Lay the formed fritters on a cookie sheet. Continue with the remaining shrimp. Chill the formed fritters in the refrigerator for 20 minutes before frying. This will allow the batter to firm so that it doesn't separate from the shrimp during cooking.

Fry the fritters: Heat the oil to 350°F (175°C) in a deep skillet. The oil should be 1½ to 2 inches (4 to 5 cm) in depth. Gently place 2 to 3 fritters in the oil and fry until golden brown on each side, 3 to 4 minutes. Dry on paper towels and serve immediately with the dipping sauce. Continue with the remaining ukoy.

UKOY DIPPING SAUCE

3 tablespoons soy sauce

½ teaspoon rice vinegar

1 teaspoon mirin

1 small clove garlic, minced

Mix all the ingredients together in a small dish. Serve with ukoy.

CHICKEN LIVER MOUSSE

Filipinos are terribly clever when it comes to inventing new uses for everyday ingredients. I am particularly fond of the use of liver in sauces and stews. Quite a few Filipino dishes call for liver or liver pâté as an ingredient, which not only imparts rich flavor but also acts as an elegant sauce thickener. Traditionally, canned liverwurst was the product of choice. However, this simple recipe far outweighs the taste and quality of a canned product and can be served in a number of ways. Alone, it is a delicious pâté served with your favorite crusty bread or sliced pears. And finally, if frozen and cut into small bouillon-sized blocks, it can be used as a flavoring or thickener in place of a traditional roux. You will be pleasantly surprised by the sultry depth that a little of this mousse will give your sauces and stews.

Makes 6 to 8 appetizer portions

2 teaspoons butter
1 yellow onion, sliced
1 clove garlic, chopped
¼ teaspoon dried thyme
¼ teaspoon ground red pepper
½ cup (125 ml) sherry
¼ lb (125 g) chicken livers
1 tablespoon soy sauce
1½ cups (375 ml) heavy
    whipping cream

Cook the livers: Melt the butter in a medium skillet (2 to 3 quarts/liters) over medium-high heat. Add the onion and cook, stirring occasionally, for 5 to 7 minutes until the onion turns golden brown. Add the garlic, dried thyme, and ground red pepper and cook another 3 minutes. Deglaze the pan with the sherry. Using a wooden spoon, scrape any of the caramelized onion bits off the bottom and sides of the pan into the sauce.

Add the livers, soy sauce, and ½ cup (125 ml) heavy cream. Reduce the heat to a simmer for 7 to 10 minutes until the mixture is almost dry and the livers are tender and fully cooked.

Remove the pan from the heat and place liver mixture in a food processor.

Prepare the mousse: Process the liver well until completely smooth. Spoon into a large bowl and set aside to cool.

Whip the remaining 1 cup (250 ml) heavy cream with an electric mixer until it reaches stiff peaks. Using a large spatula, fold the whipped cream into the cooled duck liver puree. Spoon the mixture into ramekins or a pâté crock. Chill the mousse completely in the refrigerator for at least 4 to 6 hours before serving.

ADOBO-FLAVORED PECANS

Having a drink in the Philippines always goes hand in hand with the taking of *pulutan,* the term for Filipino bar food. Simple pulutan include a wide range of dishes from grilled sweet potato *(kamote-cue)* to fried tofu *(tokwa)* to these easy-to-eat *adobo* nuts. If the salty tang of these finger-licking snacks isn't enough to tempt you, the added layer of sweet will ensure that they won't last long in your kitchen. They are wonderful as a snack, an appetizer, or as a garnish for salads.

Makes 2 cups (200 g)

2 cups (200 g) pecans (substitute peanuts, cashews, almonds, or walnuts)
3 tablespoons brown sugar
4 teaspoons soy sauce
2 teaspoons vinegar
1 teaspoon *calamansi* juice (substitute lime juice)
½ teaspoon garlic powder
½ teaspoon freshly ground black pepper

Preheat the oven to 325°F (160°C).

Combine all the ingredients in a large bowl and mix until the pecans are well coated. Pour the nuts onto a parchment-lined or lightly oiled baking sheet, separating the nuts as much as possible into a single layer. Bake for 15 minutes until the nuts are golden brown.

Cool the nuts before handling, 10 to 15 minutes. They will be crispy with a brown shiny glaze. Store in your cupboard in an airtight container for up to 2 weeks.

BEEF TURNOVERS EMPANADAS

Empanadas are a global food found in many countries under different monikers. What they all have in common is the same tidy convenience of a half-moon handheld pie. These turnovers are the classic Spanish addition to Filipino cuisine typically made with a sturdy dough that remains tender and golden when fried. This recipe offers you a baked empanada option using puff pastry dough to create a wonderfully light and flaky turnover, easily served as casual finger food or as elegant appetizers. The picadillo filling of ground beef, toasted almonds, and green olives is purposely generous; leftovers can be recycled into one of my comfort-food favorites, Arroz a la Cubana (page 85), served with rice and sweet plantains.

Makes 12 empanadas

Almondine
¼ cup (40 g) green Spanish olives
¼ cup (50 g) toasted almonds
¼ cup (40 g) raisins

Meat Filling
2 teaspoons olive oil
1 small yellow onion, diced
1 clove garlic, minced
1 lb (450 g) lean ground beef
3 tablespoons soy sauce
¾ cup (175 ml) Chicken or Beef
   Stock (see pages 15 and 14)
½ teaspoon dried oregano
½ teaspoon dried thyme
4 oz (125 g) frozen peas
1 small potato, peeled and diced
1 lb (450 g) store-bought puff
   pastry, thawed
1 large egg, beaten

Prepare the almondine: Place the green olives, almonds, and raisins in a food processor. Pulse the blade several times, until the mixture is finely chopped but not a paste. Set the mixture aside.

Cook the filling: Heat the oil in a medium sauté pan (2 to 3 quarts/liters) over medium heat. Add the onion and garlic. Cook and stir for 2 min-utes until the onion becomes translu-cent. Add the ground beef and cook for 5 to 7 minutes until well browned. Drain and discard the ren-dered fat from the pan. Add the soy sauce, stock, oregano, and thyme. Reduce the heat to a simmer for 5 to 7 minutes. Add the peas, potato, and almond mixture. Cover and simmer for another 7 to 10 minutes until the potatoes are tender. Cool the meat before filling the empanadas.

Form the empanadas: Lay the thawed sheets of puff pastry on a lightly floured surface. Using a 3⅛-inch (80-mm) round cookie cutter, cut 5 rounds of dough from each sheet. Puff pastry scraps can be cut and pressed together to form another sheet large enough to cut another 2 dough circles. Use a rolling pin to gently roll each dough circle into a slightly oval shape. Place a heaping tablespoon of meat in the center of an oval. Using a pastry brush, lightly moisten the dough's edge with water. Fold the top half of dough over the filling, lining up the edges to form a half-moon. Using the back of a fork, press the tines along the edge of the empanada to seal it shut and make a decorative edge. Repeat this process with the remaining dough. Place the finished empanadas on a baking sheet. The empanadas can be frozen at this point. Place the entire tray in the freezer for 2 to 3 hours. Once the empanadas are firm, transfer them from the baking tray to plastic freezer bags for easier storage.

Bake the empanadas: Preheat the oven to 400°F (200°C). Lightly brush the tops of the empanadas with beaten egg. Place an herb leaf, such as fresh coriander leaves (cilantro) or flat-leaf parsley, on top of each empanada as a garnish. The egg wash will "glue" the leaves to the dough. Bake for 20 to 25 minutes until the empanadas have puffed and turned golden brown.

Variation: Mushroom Empanadas. Mushrooms give the empanadas a full flavor and meaty texture without the meat. Follow the same recipe, substituting 1 pound (450 g) assorted fresh mushrooms (such as shiitake, oyster, portobello, crimini, button, chanterelles), stems removed, for the ground beef. For a truly vegetarian empanada, use vegetable broth instead of chicken broth.

FRIED SWEET BANANAS   PRITONG SAGING

There's no bad time to serve ripe pan-fried bananas. An everyday *merienda* staple, they are a perfect midmorning or midafternoon snack to wash down with coffee or hot chocolate (*tsokolate*). Easily found in Latino markets and many conventional grocery stores, the plaintain is a good substitute for the *saba,* the variety of banana used in the Philippines for Pritong Saging. The ripeness of your plantain will certainly make a notable difference in the cooked result. A hard unripe or semiripe plantain has a lot of starch and a ¼-inch (6-mm) slice will cook into a tough rubbery plank. The riper the plantain, the more its starch is replaced by sugar and you can be sure that it will fry into a tender sweet slice. As with all fried foods, serve these while they're still hot. Leftover *saging* can be chopped and sautéed with your fried rice for a natural sweetener in Arroz a la Cubana (page 85) or picadillo (page 35).

Serves 6

3 large (approximately 2 lbs/900 g) ripe but firm plantains, peeled
1 cup (250 ml) vegetable oil, for frying
½ cup (100 g) granulated sugar

Cut the bananas through the center crosswise to make short halves. Next cut the banana halves lengthwise into thirds. Continue with the remaining bananas so that you have 18 slices, roughly 3 to 4 inches (7½ to 10 cm) in length. Heat the oil in a large skillet over medium-high heat. When the oil is hot, fry the bananas 4 to 5 minutes per side until golden brown. Dry the bananas on paper towels and immediately sprinkle with the sugar while still hot.

Variation: Banana Fritters. These are dipped in a lightly sweetened batter and fried. Cut plantains the same way as when making fried bananas, per the instructions for Fried Sweet Bananas. In a bowl, combine 2 cups (275 g) all-purpose flour, 1 large egg, 1½ teaspoons baking powder, 1 teaspoon cinnamon, 1 tablespoon honey or pure maple syrup, ¼ cup (50 ml) milk, and a pinch of salt. Stir the batter until well combined. Dip the plantain slices in the batter until well coated and fry until golden brown on all sides. Dry the fried banana slices on paper towels. Serve hot.

GRILLED CHICKEN WINGS

One of Cebu City's claims to culinary fame is Carbon Market, Cebu's largest outdoor market, a claustrophobic maze of open-air and covered stalls selling everything from pristine *kangkong* (water spinach) to ocean-fresh *kuhol* (snails) or handwoven *banig* (pandan mats). Carbon is also home to multiple food stalls, one particularly that sells the most delectable grilled chicken wings with sizzled skin and smoky meat. For this recipe I've replicated those flavors with the typical *adobo* marinade proportionately stretched into a seasoned brine that will plump the wings with flavor and keep them tender as they cook over the hot coals. The kicker for these wings is the barest sprinkle of *calamansi* juice right at the end that makes each bite an explosion of flavor.

Makes approximately 25 wings

Brine
6 cups (1½ liters) boiling water
1 cup (250 ml) soy sauce
1 cup (200 g) brown sugar
1 head garlic, cut in half horizontally to expose the cloves
1 cup (250 ml) vinegar
½ cup (125 g) salt
2 bay leaves
6 cups (1½ liters) ice water

Wings
5 lbs (2¼ kg) chicken wings, approximately 25 wings
2 tablespoons sesame oil
2 teaspoons paprika
1 teaspoon freshly ground black pepper
5 to 6 fresh calamansi (substitute 1 lime), halved

Make the brine: Combine the hot water, soy sauce, brown sugar, garlic, vinegar, salt, and bay leaves in a large stockpot (7 to 8 quarts/liters). Stir to combine. Add the ice water to cool the brine. Set aside.

Prepare the chicken and marinade: Prepare the wings. Chicken wings have three sections: the large drummette, the middle section, and the wing tip. Use a sharp knife to cut between the joints, separating the wing into three parts. Reserve the wing tips for chicken stock. Place the drummette and middle sections into the cooled brine. The wings should be completely covered. Refrigerate for at least 1 hour and up to 3 hours.

Drain the wings and rinse under cold water. Pat the wings dry with paper towels. Toss the wings with sesame oil, paprika, and pepper until well coated.

Cook the wings: To cook the wings on a grill, follow Step 1; to cook them under a broiler, follow Step 2.
Step 1. Preheat the grill and oil grates. Grill the wings 5 to 7 minutes per side until cooked through. The larger drummettes may take 7 to 9 minutes per side. Place the cooked wings on a serving platter and sprinkle with squeezed calamansi or lime juice. Serve hot.

Step 2. You can achieve similar results using your broiler. Of course, your wings will lack that incomparable charcoal flavor, but substituting smoked paprika for hot paprika on the wings will give the chicken a smoky finish. Position your oven rack directly under the broiler. Preheat your broiler. Place the wings in a single layer on a baking sheet and place under the broiler for 6 to 8 minutes per side until the wings are cooked through.

Variation: Tangy Wings. For a tangy barbecue sauce to baste on your wings, combine ¼ cup (50 ml) hoisin sauce, ¼ cup (50 ml) ketchup (banana ketchup works best), 1 tablespoon honey, 1 tablespoon vinegar, and 2 teaspoons Worcestershire sauce in a bowl. Mix well and baste on wings as they cook.

STEAMED BUNS FILLED WITH CURRY CHICKEN
CURRY CHICKEN SIOPAO

I remember feeling very special as a child when my mother packed these meat-filled buns in my lunch. My class-mates were fascinated by the fluffy white snowballs that made their peanut butter and jelly sandwiches wither in comparison. Found everywhere from dim sum restaurants to roadside food stalls, *siopao* is the perfect example of how China's vast influence has integrated into everyday Filipino cuisine. These steamed buns are made with a yeast dough that can be filled with any variation of meats, poultry, fish, or vegetables to make the perfect portable snack or light meal. I recommend that any filling you use be fully cooked before forming the siopao. The final steaming of the buns is relatively short and meant only to cook the dough and heat the stuffed center.

Makes 10 Siopao

Dough
2½ tablespoons sugar
1¼ cups (300 ml) warm water
   (98 to 115°F/37 to 46°C)
2¼ teaspoons dried yeast, equivalent to 1 yeast packet
2 tablespoons olive oil
3½ cups (475 g) all-purpose flour
1 teaspoon salt

Chicken Curry Filling
1 tablespoon olive oil
1 clove garlic, minced
1 small tomato, diced
2 green onions (scallions), finely
   chopped
1 teaspoon yellow curry paste or 1½
   teaspoons curry powder
½ lb (225 g) chicken breast,
   skinned and diced
½ cup (125 ml) coconut milk
¼ cup (50 ml) Chicken Stock (see
   page 15)
1 teaspoon soy sauce
1 teaspoon shrimp paste
1 teaspoon freshly squeezed lime
   juice
2 tablespoons chopped fresh
   coriander leaves (cilantro)
Dash of freshly ground black
   pepper

Make the dough: In a small bowl, mix together the sugar, warm water, and yeast. Allow the yeast to activate for 5 minutes. The yeast should bub-ble and become foamy. Add the oil to the yeast mixture and set aside.

Combine the flour and salt in a large bowl and stir to combine. Pour the yeast mixture over the flour and mix together with a spoon until the dough comes together. Turn the dough out onto a lightly floured surface and knead the dough 5 to 6 minutes until smooth. Lightly oil the bowl and replace the dough in the center. Cover the bowl with plastic wrap or a towel and allow the dough to rest and rise in a warm place for 2 hours.

Prepare the filling: Heat the olive oil in a medium skillet (2 to 3 quarts/liters) over medium heat. Add the garlic, tomato, and green onions (scallions). Cook and stir for 2 minutes until the tomato softens. Add the curry paste, chicken, coconut milk, chicken stock, soy sauce, and shrimp paste. Cover and simmer 8 to 10 minutes until the chicken is fully cooked. Remove the cover and cook over high heat 5 to 6 minutes until the sauce thickens.

Remove from the heat and stir in the lime juice, fresh coriander leaves (cilantro), and pepper. Cool the filling for 5 minutes before filling the buns.

Form the siopao: Uncover the dough and punch it down. Turn it out onto a lightly floured surface and roll the dough into a foot-long (30-cm) log. Divide the dough into 10 pieces. Lightly cover the unused portions of dough until you are ready to use them so that they do not become dry. Take a portion of dough and using the palm of your hand press it into a 6-inch (15-cm) circle approximately ¼ inch (6 mm) thick. Place 2 tablespoons of fill-ing in the center of the dough, drawing up the sides of the circle together at the top of the bun. Pinch and twist the top to securely seal in the filling. Place the bun seamside down on a 3 by 3-inch (7½ by 7½-cm) square of wax or parchment paper. Continue this process with the remaining buns.

Cook the siopao: Arrange the buns in a steamer and steam for 12 to 15 min-utes until the buns have expanded and the centers are warm.

CRÊPES WITH SHRIMP AND GREEN PAPAYA LUMPIA SARIWA

Lumpia is the general Filipino term for "egg roll." *Sariwa* means "fresh." Together *lumpia sariwa* is a spring roll made with a delicate egg crêpe filled with any combination of meats, seafood, pickled vegetables, and herbs.

I have to admit that lumpia sariwa was never an everyday dish in our home but a specialty served at celebrations and gatherings. However, nothing more than a little organization is required to make this recipe any day of the week. I'll often have components of the dish already prepared so that when I decide to serve these delicious spring rolls, the preparation time is cut in half. The pickled vegetables can be made the week before and the crêpes can be made a month in advance, stacked between sheets of wax or parchment paper, refrigerated or frozen, and revived as needed. To revive the crêpes, steam them for a few minutes until they becomes tender and pliable before laying down the filling. The dipping sauce can be made a day ahead and reheated in the microwave. Assembly is then just a simple matter of gathering all of the ready-made components. Although the completed rolls ideally should be served immediately, they can be made up to a day ahead of time and stored in the refrigerator covered with lightly moistened paper towels and plastic wrap.

Makes 12 spring rolls

Crêpes
4 large eggs
3 tablespoons olive oil
2 cups (250 g) cornstarch
¼ teaspoon salt
2¼ cups (550 ml) water

Filling
1 small cucumber, deseeded and cut into matchsticks
1 small carrot, peeled and cut into matchsticks
½ cup (50 g) peeled and deseeded and cut into matchsticks green papayas
2 tablespoons Five-Spice Vinegar (see page 18)
2 tablespoons mirin
2 teaspoons soy sauce
½ lb (225 g) mesclun salad greens
1 cup (25 g) fresh mint leaves
1 cup (25 g) fresh coriander leaves (cilantro)
24 medium-sized shrimp, cooked and peeled
12 to 15 long chives

Make the crêpes: Combine all the crêpe ingredients in a medium bowl. Mix the batter well with a whisk. Heat an 8 or 9-inch (20–22 cm) skillet over a medium flame. Lightly grease the pan with cooking spray or an oiled paper towel. When the skillet is hot but not smoking, ladle 2 ounces (50 ml) of batter into the pan and immediately swirl the batter to evenly and completely coat the bottom of the pan. Cook the crêpe until set, 2 to 3 minutes. The edges will pull away from the side of the pan and when you firmly shake the skillet the crêpe will loosen and move freely. Using a spatula, turn the crêpe over and cook the other side, 1 to 2 minutes. Slide the crêpe onto a plate.

There is no need to re-oil the pan unless the batter from the first crêpe has stuck to it. Wipe off any stuck bits of batter. Using your ladle, stir the batter to reincorporate the cornstarch, which has a tendency to settle on the bottom of the bowl. Pour another ladle of batter into the pan and repeat the process. Stack the crêpes on top of one another until you have used all of the batter. Keep the crêpes loosely covered with a towel or plastic wrap until they have completely cooled.

Pickle the vegetables: In a large bowl toss together the cucumber, carrot, and green papaya with the vinegar, mirin, and soy sauce until well mixed. Set aside to marinate for at least 10 minutes. **Note:** If refrigerated, vegetables will store up to one week in pickling marinade.

Assemble the rolls: Place a crêpe in the center of your work surface. Lay 3 to 4 mesclun leaves in a horizontal row just below the center of the wrapper. This layer of greens will protect the crêpe from absorbing excess moisture from the marinated vegetables. Arrange a tablespoon of marinated vegetables in a row atop the salad greens. Place 2 to 3 leaves each of mint and cilantro over the vegetables. Finally place 2 pieces of shrimp on top of the herbs. Fold the bottom edge of the crêpe over the row of filling and tightly roll up the crêpe. Secure the spring roll closed by tying a chive around the center. The two ends of the roll will stay open. Place the spring roll on a platter and continue this procedure with the remaining crêpes.

Serve with traditional Lumpia Sariwa dipping sauce (page 20), a store-bought chili sauce, or the Hoisin-Tamarind Glaze (page 145).

SPICED ANCHOVY CRISPS PRITONG DILIS

Teeming off the miles of Philippine coastline are tiny anchovies called *dilis* that are dried and eaten the way all good *pulutan* finger food should be enjoyed—with plenty of beer to wash it down. It's easy to get hooked on these fried seasoned dilis that are simultaneously salty, sweet, spicy, and crunchy. Dilis are most often eaten plain with just a simple dipping sauce of vinegar or soy to add extra flavor. However, I found that combining dilis with other munchables—roasted peanuts, sunflower seeds, or even dried fruit such as banana chips—makes a uniquely addictive snack that satisfies both sweet and salt cravings (see Dilis Mix, below). You'll find a large assortment of dried anchovies at the Asian market packaged in small plastic pouches. I prefer the smaller anchovy varieties that measure 1 to 1½ inches (2½ to 3¾ cm) in length; they cook faster and fry crispier than larger anchovies.

Makes 4 ounces (125 g)
1 package (4 oz/125 g) small
   dilis, dried anchovies
1 cup (250 ml) oil, for frying
1 teaspoon lemon juice

Seasoning Mix
1 teaspoon each lemon and lime
   zest
½ teaspoon salt
½ teaspoon granulated sugar
½ teaspoon ground red pepper

In a small bowl, combine the lemon and lime zest, salt, sugar, and ground red pepper. Stir to combine. Set aside.

Heat the oil in a medium pan over high heat. When the oil is hot but not smoking, add the anchovies and fry until the anchovies are firm and evenly crisped, 3 to 5 minutes. Drain the dilis on paper towels and place in a bowl. While still hot, sprinkle the dilis first with lemon juice and then the dry seasoning mix. Toss gently to combine.

Variations: 1. Oven-Baked Dilis. Although the anchovies won't have quite the same crispiness as the deep-fried version, this oven-baked alternative leaves you with all the flavor and just a fraction of the fat.

Preheat the oven to 350°F (175°C). Toss the anchovies in a bowl with 1 teaspoon (5 ml) olive oil and season with citrus zest, salt, sugar, ground red pepper, and lemon juice. Spread the fish in a single layer on a baking sheet and bake for 25 to 30 minutes until firm and dry.

2. Smoky Dilis. To give you ample heat with the added bonus of a light, wood-smoked flavor, replace the ground red pepper in the seasoning mix with ½ teaspoon smoked paprika.

3. Dilis Mix. For a festive and original party snack, mix together 1 cup fried dilis (in your favorite flavor), ½ cup (75 g) roasted peanuts or cashews, ½ cup (50 g) dried banana chips, ½ cup (50 g) sunflower seeds, and ¼ cup (25 g) toasted coconut flakes. You might also try experimenting with toasted pumpkin seeds and dried puffed rice (*pinipig*).

WONTON SOUP PANCIT MOLO

HOT-AND-SOUR MUSHROOM SOUP MUSHROOM SINIGANG

BREAD AND CHORIZO SOUP SOPA DE PAN A LA DIABLA

CHICKEN AND RICE PORRIDGE ARROZ CALDO

MEATBALL SOUP WITH BEAN THREAD NOODLES ALMONDIGAS

SARDINE AND TOMATO NOODLE SOUP MISUA

OXTAIL AND VEGETABLE SOUP NILAGA

YOUNG COCONUT SOUP WITH CORN AND SHRIMP BINAKOL

FROG LEGS SOUP WITH GREEN PAPAYA FROG LEGS TINOLA

MUNG BEAN SOUP WITH CHORIZO AND SQUASH MONGOS

SOUPS

Other than rice, a Filipino meal needs nothing more than a good soup, or *sabaw*, to make me feel right at home. A warm bowl of *arroz caldo* rice porridge heavily scented with ginger, green onions, and chicken was a welcome aroma that often greeted me and my siblings when we arrived home from school on those frigid winter days. In my house, soup was always a vital component of our meals either as the featured main course or as an accompaniment. We'd moisten our rice with broth and eat it in tandem with the soup's meat or vegetables.

I love the versatility of Filipino soups, which range in heartiness from light broths that whet the appetite to thick stews that quickly fill the belly with just a few spoonfuls. Two styles of soup that, despite the occupation of two Western cultures, haven't made their way onto the Filipino table are creamed and pureed soups. For this collection I've selected an eclectic assortment of soups—including a nontraditional mushroom variation of arroz caldo—that gives you the versatility to choose between a one-pot meal, a casual side dish, or an elegant first course.

I can't definitively say that there is a quintessential Filipino soup the way *adobo* or *pancit* are considered national dishes, eaten in some variation all over the islands. However, there is one class of soup called *sinigang*, a term used for sour broth soups, used to stimulate the appetite and cool the body from the tropical island heat. The components may vary from seafood, meats, or vegetables with the souring agent traditionally represented by a fruit such as *calamansi* (native lime), tamarind, or green mango. Native vinegars, like those distilled from coconut water, sugarcane, or palm sap, are also a popular souring alternative being less acidic than the distilled white or cider vinegars commonly used in the United States. Regardless of the ingredients you wish to highlight in your soup, whether they be sweet scallops, creamy *buko* (tender coconut meat), or aromatic oxtail, sinigang demonstrates the care that Filipinos take in balancing the soup's acidity so that it melts with the other flavors into a lively harmonious broth.

Despite having been fully integrated into Filipino cuisine, many of the soups have maintained characteristics of their national origins. Though Spanish in name, Arroz Caldo (chicken and rice soup) bears all the traits of thick porridgelike congee from China. Spain's contributions are reflected in Sopa de Pan a la Diabla and meatball soup or Almondigas, "Filipinoed" by the addition of bean thread noodles. Other soups, such as Binakol with its young coconut meat, the heavily gingered Tinola, and a simple boiled oxtail and vegetable soup called Nilaga, bear the original Malay flavors.

Creating a superior soup is no different than with any other recipe—it starts with good quality ingredients, at the core of which is stock. A Filipino kitchen is incomplete without a light chicken stock used to add moisture, delicate flavor, and body to almost any dish—from soups to stews to stir-fries—without overpowering the flavor of other ingredients. However, I oftentimes prefer matching my stock to the main ingredient in my recipes for more intense flavor: chicken stock for chicken or pork dishes; beef stock for beef dishes; fish or shrimp stock for seafood dishes; vegetable stock for vegetables. The Basics chapter includes simple recipes for beef, chicken, seafood, and vegetable stocks to suit your specific needs.

I highly suggest reading and trying the recipe variations to give yourself options in preparing and flavoring your soup so that it best suits your needs. Often even the smallest changes in procedure or seasoning can be the difference between a recipe that you never try and one that becomes your all-time favorite.

WONTON SOUP PANCIT MOLO

The name of this soup is somewhat deceiving. Those familiar with *pancit* know that it normally falls under the category of Filipino noodles. However, Pancit Molo is the exception. Noodles are replaced by wontons in this light soup from the Molo district of Iloilo, one of the four provinces composing the Visayan island of Panay. The wontons admittedly take some time to form, but this recipe will leave you with enough to freeze for a quick soup during the week. For a shortcut, form the meatballs out of the filling and cook them in the broth. Cut the wonton wrappers into strips and add them to the soup for instant noodles.

Serves 4
Makes 32 to 36 wontons
Wontons
½ lb (225 g) ground pork
2 teaspoons peeled and minced
    fresh ginger
1 green onion (scallion), finely
    chopped
1 tablespoon soy sauce
1 teaspoon freshly ground black
    pepper
1 package (10 oz/275 g/50 pieces)
    round wonton wrappers
1 large egg, beaten

Broth
4 cups (1 liter) Chicken Stock (see
    page 15)
One 1-in (2½-cm) piece fresh ginger,
    peeled
One 1-in (2½-cm) piece lemon-
    grass
2 tablespoons fish sauce
Pinch of freshly ground black pepper
1 green onion (scallion), chopped
¼ lb (125 g) watercress, washed,
    with woody stems removed

Form the wontons: Combine the ground pork, ginger, green onion (scallion), soy sauce, and black pepper in a bowl. Mix the ingredients thoroughly. Place a wonton wrapper on your work surface. Use a pastry brush to lightly moisten the edges of the wrapper with beaten egg. Place a teaspoon of meat filling in the center of the wrapper. Fold the top half of the wonton over the filling so that the edges meet to form a half-moon. Press out any air bubbles around the filling and firmly seal the edges. Lightly moisten one corner of the half-moon and fold it around the belly of filling to meet the other corner. The dumpling will look like a bishop's hat. Press the corners together firmly and place upright on a baking sheet. Continue with the remaining wontons.

Make the soup: Combine the chicken stock, ginger, lemongrass, and fish sauce in a large pot. Simmer the broth over medium-low heat for 15 to 20 minutes. Remove and discard the ginger and lemongrass. Add 12 to 15 wontons to the soup and simmer for 5 to 6 minutes until the wontons are completely cooked. Turn off the heat and stir in the chopped green onion (scallion) and watercress. Ladle the soup into bowls and serve hot.

HOT-AND-SOUR MUSHROOM SOUP MUSHROOM SINIGANG

There is nothing more satisfying than the smooth tang and suggestive burn of a harmonious hot-and-sour soup. *Sinigang* is the general term used for sour broth soups that are altogether bright and refreshing, often with a chile kick. Traditionally soured with fruit such as *calamansi* (Filipino lime), tamarind, or green mango, native vinegars distilled from coconut water, palm sap, or sugarcane are also used as mild souring agents, being less acidic than the distilled white or cider vinegars used in the United States. In this recipe, mushrooms really shine, their earthy flavor a natural complement to the clean broth. A healthy mix of dried and fresh mushrooms gives this soup maximum flavor and weighty texture.

Serves 4
4 to 5 dried shiitake mushrooms
One ½-oz (15-g) piece fresh ginger, peeled
5 cups (1¼ liters) water
1 bay leaf
1 small Thai chile, stem removed
½ lb (225 g) fresh assorted mushrooms (such as shiitake, chanterelle, oyster, enoki), sliced
1 clove garlic, minced
1 small tomato, deseeded and diced
3 tablespoons palm or coconut vinegar
1 teaspoon soy sauce
Pinch of ground black pepper
3 calamansi, halved

Reconstitute the dried mushrooms: Place the dried mushrooms, ginger, water, bay leaf, and chile in a large pot. Simmer over low heat for 15 minutes. Remove the mushrooms, ginger, bay leaf, and chile from the broth, discarding all but the mushrooms. Cut off and discard the mushroom stems. Slice the tender caps into thin strips and return to the pot.

Make the soup: Add the sliced fresh mushrooms, garlic, tomato, vinegar, soy sauce, and pepper. Simmer for 10 minutes until the mushrooms are tender. Ladle the soup into bowls and serve with the calamansi.

BREAD AND CHORIZO SOUP SOPA DE PAN A LA DIABLA

Full of caramelized onion flavor, this bread soup bears a strong resemblance to French onion soup; added character is lent by chorizo de Bilbao, a semicured sausage heavily seasoned with paprika, which gives the soup a spicy piquant element. Any Spanish-style, semicured sausage will impart an irresistible richness to this light soup. Because bread is one of the main ingredients, use a well-made artisanal bread to make firm dense croutons that maintain their shape and texture once added to the soup. Though not a Filipino standard, I've grown fond of making my croutons from either sourdough bread or French baguettes. For a healthy alternative, try this *sopa* with whole wheat or multigrain croutons.

Serves 4

3 cups (125 g) day-old bread cut
  into ½-in (1⅓-cm) cubes
½ teaspoon smoked paprika
¼ cup (50 ml) olive oil
¼ teaspoon salt
1 tablespoon unsalted butter
1 onion, sliced
¼ cup (25 g) sliced chorizo de Bilbao
¼ cup (50 ml) rice wine
3 cups (750 ml) Beef Stock (see
  page 14)
¼ teaspoon dried oregano
Salt and freshly ground black pepper
  to taste

Make the croutons: Preheat the oven to 300°F (150°C). Combine the bread cubes, paprika, olive oil, and salt in a large bowl. Toss the ingredients to evenly distribute the spices. Spread the bread evenly on a baking sheet and bake for 20 to 25 minutes, until bread is completely firm and toasted. Remove from the oven and cool. Set aside.

Make the soup: Heat the butter in a medium pot (3 quarts/liters) over medium heat. Add the onion and cook for 8 to 10 minutes, stirring occasionally, until the onion caramelizes and turns golden brown. Add the chorizo de Bilbao and cook for another 2 minutes. Add the rice wine, beef stock, and oregano.

Simmer for 15 to 20 minutes to marry the flavors. Season with salt and pepper. Ladle the soup into bowls, sprinkle soup with croutons, and serve immediately.

CHICKEN AND RICE PORRIDGE ARROZ CALDO

Arroz caldo bears a Spanish name that translates into "rice soup," but this dish is 100 percent Chinese in origin and directly descended from congee. Most Filipinos know arroz caldo (also called *pospas* or *lugaw*) as a thick, hearty rice porridge heavily infused with ginger and flavored with stewed chicken. Using bone-in chicken parts will give your soup more flavor than using boneless chicken breast. Going this route means that arroz caldo is best eaten with a spoon and fork to maneuver the tender chicken off the bone. If you want to enjoy the convenience of boneless chicken, substitute cooked, shredded chicken instead of whole parts. Your soup will be delicious, without the added work of the fork. The traditional garnish is a sprinkle of toasted garlic, a special touch that really makes this soup memorable.

Serves 6

Toasted Garlic Garnish
¼ cup (50 ml) olive oil
3 cloves garlic, chopped

Soup
2 lbs (900 g) skinless bone-in chicken
   thighs or legs
One 1-oz (25-g) piece fresh ginger,
   peeled
2 green onions (scallions)
2 cloves garlic, minced
2 tablespoons soy sauce
8 cups (2 liters) Chicken Stock (see
   page 15)
1 cup (200 g) uncooked long-grain
   rice
Salt and freshly ground black pepper
   to taste

Toast the garlic: Heat the olive oil in a small skillet over medium-low heat. Add the garlic and cook for 3 to 5 minutes, stirring frequently, until the garlic is a light golden brown. Place a fine sieve over a bowl and strain the garlic. Dry the garlic on paper towels and cool. Cool the oil and reserve for later use.

Make the soup: Place the chicken, ginger, green onions (scallions), garlic, and soy sauce into a large (4 to 5-quart/liter) pot. Pour the chicken broth into the pot and bring the soup to a boil. Reduce the heat to low-medium and simmer for 20 minutes. Add the rice to the soup and simmer for another 30 minutes, stirring the rice to assure it does not stick to the bottom of the pot. The soup is ready when it becomes very thick and the rice is tender. Season with salt and pepper. Ladle the soup into bowls and sprinkle with the toasted garlic.

Variation: Mushroom Arroz Caldo.
For a vegetarian alternative, a mixture of dried and fresh mushrooms makes an intense flavorful soup. Soak 3 to 4 dried shiitake mushrooms or ½ cup (15 g) dried porcini mushrooms in 4 cups (1 liter) hot water for 20 minutes until mushrooms soften. Slice the reconstituted shiitake mushrooms thinly. Combine the ginger, green onions (scallions), garlic, shiitake mushrooms, 1 pound (450 g) sliced fresh mushrooms (your choice), mushroom soaking liquid, soy sauce, and 4 cups (1 liter) water in a pot and simmer for 15 minutes. Add 1 cup (200 g) rice and simmer for another 25 minutes until the rice is tender. Adjust the seasonings and serve with the toasted garlic. For extra mushroom flavor, drizzle a little truffle oil on top of the soup before serving.

MEATBALL SOUP WITH BEAN THREAD NOODLES ALMONDIGAS

It may not be glamorous or fancy, but this meatball and noodle soup is a satisfying weekday treasure. The noodles used for this dish are bean thread noodles, or *sotanghon*, and the meatballs are a savory combination of seasoned pork and shrimp. Sotanghon are dried, wiry, transparent noodles made from mung bean starch. Often found under different monikers, you might find them labeled cellophane noodles, glass noodles, or mung bean vermicelli. Sotanghon are dried in tight bundles made up of long noodle strands, which can be difficult to cut or separate. Soak the noodles first in warm water for 5 to 7 minutes to soften, then cut them into more manageable lengths. They cook quickly in hot liquid and add an enjoyable slick texture to the broth.

Serves 4

Meatballs

4 to 5 jumbo shrimp, peeled and deveined

½ lb (225 g) ground pork

2 cloves garlic, minced

2 tablespoons Japanese panko bread crumbs

1 green onion (scallion), finely chopped, white and green parts separated

1 chicken bouillon cube, crushed into a powder

Soup

1 tablespoon olive oil

1 large shallot, chopped

½ small red bell pepper, seeded and chopped

2 tablespoons tomato paste

5 cups (1¼ liters) Beef Stock (see page 14)

2 tablespoons soy sauce

1-oz (25-g) bundle bean thread noodles, soaked in warm water

Make the meatballs: Place the shrimp in a food processor. Pulse several times until well chopped into a paste. In a large bowl, combine the shrimp paste, ground pork, garlic, bread crumbs, finely chopped white part of the green onion (scallion), and crushed bouillon cube. Mix thoroughly. Using the palms of your hands, roll a heaping tablespoon of the meat mixture into balls approximately ½ inch (1¼ cm) in diameter. Place the formed balls on a tray. Continue with the remaining meat. Keep the meatballs in the refrigerator until ready to use. Makes 16 to 20 meatballs.

Make the soup: Heat the olive oil in a large pot over medium heat. Add the shallot and red pepper. Cook and stir for 2 to 3 minutes until the shallot becomes translucent. Add the tomato paste, beef stock, and soy sauce. Bring the soup to a simmer. Carefully drop the meatballs into the pot. Simmer another 7 to 9 minutes: the meatballs will float to the surface. Remove bean thread noodles from soaking liquid and add to the pot. Discard the soaking liquid. Simmer the soup for another 5 minutes until the noodles are tender. Ladle the soup into bowls and garnish with the finely chopped green part of the green onion (scallion).

SARDINE AND TOMATO NOODLE SOUP MISUA

Although my dad was not as proficient in the kitchen as my mom, when he pulled dinner duty he always managed to satisfy us with this delicious, lightning-quick soup. A generation later, *misua* has become one of my daughter's favorite dishes and a weekday special in our home that even my husband can manage with ease. Sardines are a staple on the islands and enjoyed with equal enthusiasm in their many forms: fresh, dried, or canned. For this recipe, sardines packed in tomato sauce are the key ingredient and can easily be substituted with fresh sardines and fresh tomato sauce when either is in season. Misua noodles are specific to Filipino cuisine and will definitely warrant a trip to the Asian market. They are fragile, superfine wheat noodles that cook in a matter of seconds. Once cooked, they have a silky, melt-in-your-mouth texture unlike any other noodle.

Serves 4

1 tablespoon olive oil
2 cloves garlic, minced
1 green onion (scallion), chopped, white bulb and green stalk separated
1 small tomato, diced
2 (5½-oz/150-g) cans sardines in tomato sauce
3 cups (750 ml) Chicken Stock (see page 15)
2 oz (50 g) misua noodles
2 teaspoons fish sauce

Heat the olive oil in a medium pot (2 to 3 quarts/liters) over medium heat. Add the garlic, the white part of the green onion (scallion), and the tomato. Cook and stir for 2 to 3 minutes until the tomato begins to soften.

Add the canned sardines with the tomato sauce and chicken stock. Simmer the soup for 5 minutes. Add the misua noodles, fish sauce, and pepper. Simmer another 5 minutes until the noodles soften and the soup thickens. Ladle the soup into bowls and garnish with the chopped green spring onion (scallion). Serve immediately.

OXTAIL AND VEGETABLE SOUP NILAGA

This soup became a staple for me in college when I left behind my freshman diet of pizza and instant noodles and eventually had to fend for myself in the kitchen. In the eighties, before it graduated into the galleys of haute cuisine, oxtail was a cheap beef cut that fit perfectly into my meager budget and cooked well in my favorite piece of kitchen equipment, the slow cooker. It's no wonder that *nilaga* altogether suited my student sensibilities. I'd start frozen oxtail with water in the morning before I left for class and the meat would be falling off the bone in a concentrated broth by the time I returned home. If you cannot get oxtail, crosscut beef shanks cook marvelously. The tender meat and precious marrow are just rewards for a hearty appetite.

Serves 4

1½ lbs (675 g) oxtail, cut into 1 to 2-in (25 to 50-mm) pieces (substitute beef shank)
7 cups (1¼ liters) water
1 bay leaf
One ½-oz (15-g) slice fresh ginger, peeled
2 garlic gloves, peeled
2 tablespoons fish sauce
1 teaspoon coconut or palm vinegar
1 small leek, cleaned and sliced
¼ lb (125 g) Chinese long beans, cut into 3-in (7½-cm) pieces
2 oz (50 g) horseradish leaves

Place the oxtail, water, bay leaf, ginger, and garlic into a large pot (4 to 5 quarts/liters). Bring the water to a boil. Using a ladle, skim and discard any foam that floats to the surface.

Lower the heat, cover, and simmer for 2½ to 3 hours until the beef is very tender and easily pulls away from the bone. Season the broth with the fish sauce and vinegar. Add the leek and beans and simmer for another 5 minutes.

Turn off the heat. Remove and discard the bay leaf. Stir in the horseradish leaves and allow 2 minutes for it to cook before serving. Ladle into bowls and serve immediately.

YOUNG COCONUT SOUP WITH CORN AND SHRIMP BINAKOL

So important is coconut in the Philippines that there are over a dozen different Filipino words for it in its various forms and uses. *Binakol* is a pre-Hispanic soup that traces its roots to the Malay natives and features *buko* (young coconut meat). Unlike meat from the brown-shelled, mature coconut that is semidry and hard, buko is very moist and tender like a cooked apple or a ripe pear. Featured with fresh sweet corn and shrimp, binakol is the perfect summer soup to enjoy with a simple salad or light entrée. To maximize the soup's corn flavor I make an intense broth out of the cobs, which are packed with corn goodness. You won't be sorry you made the extra effort. If you're using frozen kernels and don't have cobs to make broth, vegetable or chicken stock make delicious stand-ins. Buko is available in Asian markets canned in a light syrup or plainly frozen in thin chunks.

Serves 6

Corn Broth: makes 6½ cups (1⅔ liters)
1 tablespoon butter
1 onion, chopped
2 cloves garlic, peeled
1 bay leaf
A few strands of saffron
3 large ears sweet corn, kernels cut off cobs (reserve kernels for soup)
7 cups (1½ liters) water

Binakol
1 teaspoon olive oil
½ cup (150 g) thinly sliced leeks
2 tablespoons rice wine
1 cup (125 g) fresh corn kernels
1 can (20 oz/570 g) young coconut meat, buko, drained and thinly sliced
5 cups (1¼ liters) corn broth (substitute Vegetable or Chicken Stock, see page 15)
3 tablespoons fish sauce
¼ teaspoon white pepper
½ lb (225 g) shrimp, peeled and deveined
1 small lime, thinly sliced
1 tablespoon chopped fresh coriander leaves (cilantro)

Make the corn broth: Heat the butter in a large pot (4 to 5 quarts/liters) over medium-high heat. Add the onion. Cook and stir for 3 to 4 minutes, until the onion starts to brown. Add the garlic, bay leaf, saffron, corn cobs, and water. Bring the broth to a simmer. While the broth is simmering, begin assembling and preparing the other ingredients for Binakol. After 30 minutes, remove the broth from the heat. Strain the broth through a fine sieve discarding the vegetables and aromatics. Reserve the broth for soup.

Make the soup: Heat the olive oil in a medium pot (3 to 4 quarts/liters) over a medium flame. Add the leeks. Cook and stir the leeks 3 to 4 minutes until they start to brown. Add the rice wine and cook until almost evaporated. Add the corn kernels, sliced coconut meat, corn broth, fish sauce, and white pepper. Bring the soup to a simmer for 7 to 10 minutes. Add the shrimp and simmer for another 3 to 4 minutes until the shrimp are fully cooked. Ladle the soup into bowls with a slice of lime, sprinkle soup with chopped fresh coriander leaves (cilantro), and serve immediately.

Variation: Binakol Chowder. Start off the soup as originally directed, sautéing the leeks and deglazing the pan with rice wine. Add the corn kernels, broth, fish sauce, and white pepper. Reserve the coconut meat. Simmer the soup for 15 to 20 minutes until the corn is tender. Use a blender to puree the soup in batches until creamy. Return the soup to the pot and bring to a simmer. Add the coconut meat and shrimp and simmer for another 5 to 6 minutes. Adjust the seasonings and serve with lime and fresh coriander leaves (cilantro) garnishes.

I'm sure that for many, the title of this dish is enough to warrant skipping right over it and moving on to the next recipe. But don't let your greenness with frog legs discourage you from enjoying this highly underrated meat that is a surprising delight to neophytes. The adage that "they taste like chicken" is a testament to frog legs' unassuming flavor and familiar texture that won't take you far from your culinary comfort zone—especially as featured here, in this *tinola*, a common Filipino soup and one of my all-time favorites traditionally made with chicken or fish. The broth, perfumed by herbaceous lemongrass, green papaya, and ginger, is the perfect milieu for the delicate flavor of frog legs, making this clean fresh soup an irresistible pleasure. Frog legs are available fresh at Asian markets or frozen in the seafood section. They require little or no preparation and come ready to cook for easy convenience. If frog legs are unavailable to you, use chicken breast or sea scallops as a substitute.

Serves 4

1 tablespoon olive oil

1 lb (450 g) frog legs, approximately 8 pairs, separated

¼ cup (25 g) all-purpose flour

¼ cup (50 ml) rice wine

1 tablespoon peeled and minced fresh ginger

1 stalk lemongrass, cut into 2-in (5-cm) pieces

5 cups (1¼ liters) Chicken Stock (see page 15)

2 cups (200 g) peeled, deseeded, and sliced green papaya

¼ cup (25 g) lycium dried berries

2 tablespoons fish sauce

¼ teaspoon freshly ground black pepper

1 small bunch watercress, washed with woody stems removed

Heat the olive oil in a large sauté pan (3 to 4 quarts/liters) over medium-high heat. Dredge the frog legs in the flour, shaking off any excess. When the pan is hot, place the frog legs in the pan and sear for 3 to 4 minutes per side until the meat is well browned.

Depending on the size of your frog legs, you may have to do this in two batches, setting the first batch on a plate while the second cooks. Once all the frog legs are seared, return them to the pan and add the rice wine, scraping off any caramelized bits on the bottom of the pan.

Add the ginger, lemongrass, and chicken broth and simmer for 15 minutes. Add the green papaya, lycium, fish sauce, and pepper.

Simmer another 5 minutes until the green papaya is tender. Turn off the heat and stir in the watercress. Ladle the soup into bowls and serve hot.

MUNG BEAN SOUP WITH CHORIZO AND SQUASH MONGOS

Beans are not a dietary staple in the Philippines except for the regular appearance of the healthy, delicious, and versatile mung bean. Originally from India, these tiny olive green beans (or mustard yellow, if shelled and split in half) have crossed the continents, gaining popularity in Western grocery stores in their germinated form, the bean sprout. But the dried bean itself should not be neglected, being a nutritious, flavorful, and quick-cooking alternative to other legumes. *Mongos* is packed with the hearty flavors of Spanish-style chorizo and butternut squash, the perfect remedy to ward off winter's stubborn chill.

Serves 6

1 tablespoon olive oil
2 cloves garlic, minced
1 teaspoon peeled and minced fresh ginger
1 green onion (scallion), finely chopped
1 small tomato, diced
¼ lb (125 g) diced chorizo de Bilbao (substitute andouille or kielbasa sausage)
½ cup (100 g) dried green mung beans
¼ lb (125 g) butternut squash, peeled, deseeded, and cut into ½-in (1¼-cm) cubes
4 cups (1 liter) Chicken Stock (see page 15)
1 tablespoon soy sauce
Pinch of freshly ground black pepper
3 oz (75 g) spinach leaves, cleaned, stems removed

Heat the olive oil in a medium pot (2 to 3 quarts/liters) over medium heat. Add the garlic, ginger, green onion (scallion), and tomato. Cook and stir for 2 minutes. Add the chorizo de Bilbao and cook for another minute. Add the mung beans, squash, and chicken stock. Cover the pot and lower the heat. Simmer the mung beans for 45 minutes until the mung beans are plump and tender. Be careful not to overcook the beans, which tend to become mushy when overdone.

Season the soup with soy sauce and pepper. Turn off the heat, stir in the spinach, and cover the pot. Allow 2 minutes for the spinach to wilt before serving. Ladle the soup into bowls and serve immediately.

PICKLED GREEN MANGOES AND JACKFRUIT

FIVE-SPICE PICKLED VEGETABLES ACHARA

MARINATED SCALLOPS WITH PINEAPPLE AND COCONUT CREAM SCALLOP KILAW

GREEN PAPAYA AND JICAMA SALAD SINKAMAS

CUCUMBER AND TOMATO SALAD

GRILLED SQUID WITH CHORIZO AND OLIVES PUSIT SALAD

WATER SPINACH SALAD WITH SESAME DRESSING

PALM HEARTS AND APPLE SALAD WITH CALAMANSI MAYONNAISE

MARINATED SALMON SALAD WITH FENNEL SALMON KILAW

PICKLES AND SALADS

Filipinos are vinegar junkies. In fact, vinegar tops the seasoning hierarchy at number three, after salt (soy or fish sauce are salt equivalents) and black pepper as a way of simultaneously flavoring and preserving many cooked and uncooked foods. Since lettuces are not a substantive crop grown on the islands, pickled vegetables and local greens, collectively called *achara*, are the Filipino answer to salad and are offered on the table as a refreshing condiment to the main dish, transforming plain steamed rice into a substantive meal or adorning heavier viands of meat or fish. This chapter includes a delicious, goes-with-everything achara of jicama, green papaya, and daikon radish flavored with a subtle harmony of five-spice infused vinegar. With just a touch of sweetness, this achara is surprisingly versatile as an exciting and healthy accompaniment to grilled fish, broiled chicken, or even a juicy burger.

Also included is a sweet-tart pickle of green mangoes and jackfruit, a remarkable combination of two super-charged fruits that will knock your socks off. My lettuce-loving sensibility has compelled me to include one "saladesque" dish in this chapter, the Sinkamas Salad with green papaya, jicama, and watercress paired with an almond-pear vinaigrette, admittedly a crossroads combination of Eastern ingredients and Western techniques.

Walking through Cebu's outdoor food markets in the Philippines is a cook's dream, a visual bombardment of fresh fruits and vegetables that compel locals and tourists alike to buy, eat, and enjoy nature's bounty. Staples of mangoes, sweet corn, tomatoes, eggplant, and water spinach invite simple preparation for their flavors to shine. The Cucumber and Tomato Salad is a mid- to late-summer favorite, when my garden spits out juicy tomatoes faster than I can use them. Simple and satisfying, this salad gets meaty with slices of buffalo mozzarella and a sunny citrus-anchovy dressing, making it a meal in itself. You'll be pleasantly surprised by the Water Spinach Salad that pairs crunchy water spinach stems *kangkong* with bean sprouts in a spicy sesame dressing for an addictive side dish. With forests of coconut palms covering the islands, fresh *ubod* (palm hearts) are a common delicacy. Here they are featured with the herbaceous bite of Chinese celery and clean tang of tart Granny Smith apples, a winning combination that makes a compelling alternative to your standard coleslaw.

With over seven thousand islands making up the Philippine archipelago, the seas surrounding the islands are the veins through which the lifeblood of the Philippines flows. It is only natural that seafood plays a primary role in the Filipino diet and is enjoyed with zeal and creativity. *Kinilaw* or *kilaw* is the ancient practice of lightly "cooking" only the freshest seafood without heat in an acidic marinade such as tamarind, citrus, or vinegar merely to firm the texture and infuse the flavor. Included in this chapter are two very friendly kilaw recipes— Salmon Kilaw and Scallop Kilaw—full of flavor and balance, which use coconut cream to tame the acidic edge into a smooth vibrant finish. The Salmon Kilaw is paired with a shaved fennel salad for another layer of subtle anise flavor atop the five-spice vinegar used to marinate the fish. In the Scallop Kilaw, sweet pineapple and red bell peppers make an irresistible sweet-sour trio served on toasted bread or crispy rice cakes. Also featured is a fantastic grilled squid salad flavored with Spanish chorizo and olives that your guests won't soon forget.

PICKLED GREEN MANGOES AND JACKFRUIT

For Filipinos, nothing beats the sweet juicy indulgence of a perfectly ripe mango, except perhaps for the tart bite of a green mango. Green mangoes are prized on the Islands for their sour flavor and firm texture, which makes them a versatile souring ingredient in soups, stir-fries, and pickles. Green mangoes are even gobbled up with nothing more than a dab of salty *bagoong* shrimp paste to make a snack as popular on the Islands as potato chips are in the States. In this recipe I've paired green mangoes with the incomparable flavor of jackfruit for a pickle that is both sour and sweet. This savvy relish, shown opposite, is a delightful partner for grilled poultry or fish and even gives burgers new possibilities.

Serves 6

2 green mangoes, peeled and sliced
into ½-in (1⅓-cm) batons
1 (20-oz/570-g) can jackfruit,
drained and sliced, reserve syrup
for pickling liquid

Pickling Liquid
½ cup (125 ml) palm or coconut
vinegar
¾ cup (175 ml) jackfruit syrup,
reserved from canned jackfruit
½ cup (125 ml) water
1 teaspoon salt

½ teaspoon black peppercorns
1 bay leaf
1 small *sili labuyo* (Thai chile),
chopped
One ½-in (1⅓-cm) slice fresh ginger,
peeled
One 2-in (5-cm) piece lemongrass,
smashed to release its essence

Fill a 1-quart/liter preserving jar with sliced mangoes and jackfruit.

Combine the ingredients for the pickling liquid in a small saucepan. Simmer for 15 minutes to marry the flavors. Strain the liquid into a bowl and pour into the jar with the mangoes and jackfruit, making sure that the fruit are completely submerged in the pickling liquid. Cool to room temperature and refrigerate. Chill for 24 hours before serving. Keeps in the refrigerator for 3 to 4 weeks.

FIVE-SPICE PICKLED VEGETABLES ACHARA

Achara follows the Filipino pattern of being both a specific dish as well as a cooking technique. It refers to the pickling of any variety of fruits or vegetables in native souring agents, which may include palm vinegar, tamarind, or *calamansi*, a citrus fruit similar to lime. Here I've opted to use a five-spice infused vinegar that will add body and dimension to the tang. I keep a pickle jar of achara in my refrigerator at all times to add instant texture and flavor contrast to grilled fish, meat, or chicken, similar to a relish or salsa. A mandoline or vegetable slicer is just the tool to create long, matchstick strips in a flash.

Serves 6
Achara
1 small carrot, peeled and cut into
matchsticks
4 small radishes, cut into matchsticks
¼ lb (125 g) green papaya, peeled,
deseeded, and cut into matchsticks
¼ lb (125 g) jicama, peeled and
cut into matchsticks
1 small red onion, thinly sliced

Vinaigrette: makes 1½ cups (375 ml)
½ cup (125 ml) Five-Spice Vinegar
(see page 18)

1 cup (250 ml) water
¼ cup (50 g) sugar
½ teaspoon peeled and minced fresh
ginger
1 teaspoon salt
Juice of 1 lime
Pinch of dried red pepper flakes

Prepare the vegetables: Combine the carrot, radishes, green papaya, jicama, and red onion in a large bowl. Toss to combine.

Make the vinaigrette: Combine all the ingredients in a small pot over medium heat and simmer for 3 minutes. Stir to ensure that all of the sugar has dissolved. Pour the hot vinaigrette over the shredded vegetables, pressing down the vegetables so that they are submerged in the liquid. Cool to room temperature before serving. Store the achara in an airtight container with pickling liquid in the refrigerator for up to 3 weeks.

MARINATED SCALLOPS WITH PINEAPPLE AND COCONUT CREAM
SCALLOP KILAW

Kilaw, or *kinilaw*, is what Edilberto Alegre and Doreen Fernandez describe in their book *Kinilaw* as cooking with liquid fire. It is the culinary term for a technique that requires using only the freshest fish, meats, or vegetables and briefly applying a condiment of native vinegar or acid just until the food is barely past raw. Although similar to Mexican seviche in principle, kilaw is an ancient cooking method in the Philippines that predates the Spaniards who brought many Mexican elements to the islands. This kilaw is different in that the coconut cream tames much of the acidic edge. Serve this kilaw plain, accompanied by a salad, or on toast as an appetizer. The Hoisin-Tamarind Glaze (page 145) and a little of the spicy sambal ulek are the perfect sauces to garnish the kilaw for an added layer of zing.

1 lb (450 g) bay scallops (substitute chopped sea scallops)
1½ cups (375 ml) Five-Spice Vinegar (see page 18)
1 lime, zest and juice
1 small red bell pepper, finely diced
1 cup (175 g) finely diced fresh pineapple
1 green onion (scallion), finely chopped
¼ cup (50 ml) Coconut Cream (see page 16)
¼ teaspoon salt
Pinch of freshly ground black pepper

Combine the scallops, five-spice vinegar, and lime zest and juice together in a nonreactive container. Marinate for 30 minutes in the refrigerator. Drain and discard all the liquid from the scallops.

Toss the scallops in a bowl with the red bell pepper, pineapple, green onion (scallion), coconut cream, salt, and pepper until well mixed. Chill for 1 hour before serving.

GREEN PAPAYA AND JICAMA SALAD SINKAMAS

Lettuces and salad greens have never been a traditional component of a Filipino meal. But this hybrid salad is reminiscent of the achara pickles that Filipinos prefer as an accompaniment to their main dishes. The clean flavors of jicama *sinkamas* and green papaya are united with watercress for a combination that is both vibrant and herbaceous. The almond-pear vinaigrette is a European import that reflects my affinity for oil-based salad dressings, a nonexistent condiment in Filipino cuisine. A few drops of pure almond extract and pear juice go a long way to add loads of fresh flavor without a tremendous amount of oil. The vinaigrette is also a versatile dressing, terrific for coleslaw or as a dipping sauce for fresh vegetables.

Serves 6

Almond-Pear Vinaigrette: makes 1¾ cups (425 ml)

1 pear, peeled and cored
1 (6-oz/180-ml) can pear juice or pear nectar
¼ cup (50 ml) plus 2 teaspoons palm vinegar (substitute rice vinegar)
¼ teaspoon pure almond extract
1 clove garlic, peeled
¼ teaspoon peeled and chopped fresh ginger
¼ cup (50 ml) extra virgin olive oil
½ teaspoon salt
Freshly ground black pepper to taste

Salad

½ lb (225 g) jicama, peeled and cut into matchsticks
½ lb (225 g) green papaya, peeled, deseeded, and cut into matchsticks
1 bunch watercress, rinsed, woody stems removed
½ cup (100 g) toasted almonds
1 pear, thinly sliced
¼ teaspoon toasted black sesame seeds
Salt and freshly ground pepper to taste

Prepare the vinaigrette: Place all of the vinaigrette ingredients in a blender. Blend for 1 to 2 minutes until smooth. Store in the refrigerator in an airtight container for up to 1 week.

Make the salad: Combine the shredded jicama, green papaya, and watercress in a large salad bowl. Pour ½ cup (125 ml) of the almond-pear vinaigrette over the salad. Season with salt and pepper and gently toss. Sprinkle the almonds over the salad. Garnish with pear slices and a sprinkling of black sesame seeds on top.

CUCUMBER AND TOMATO SALAD

Summer could hardly pass in Chicago without leaving in its wake overflowing spoils of tomatoes in every variety and color. Leave it to Mother Nature to provide the bulk of the flavor in this dish by choosing the freshest ripest tomatoes of the season. In the Philippines *kesong puti*, a soft-ripened cheese made from fermented caribou milk, is the native cheese enjoyed with this dish for its sweet creaminess and tangy finish. Pure buffalo mozzarella mimics the flavor and texture of *kesong puti* for an excellent stand-in. The anchovy dressing features *bagoong balayan*, a fermented anchovy sauce found in the condiments section of Asian markets. Canned anchovy fillets can be used in a crunch, although your dressing won't have the unique flavor print characteristic of Southeast Asia.

Serves 4

Citrus-Anchovy Dressing: makes
¼ cup (50 ml)
¼ cup (50 ml) olive oil
2 tablespoons calamansi juice
1 tablespoon chopped green onion
(scallion)
1 clove garlic, peeled
2 teaspoons bagoong balayan
(anchovy paste) or 2 fillets canned
anchovies
1 tablespoon chopped fresh coriander leaves (cilantro)
½ teaspoon sugar
Salt and freshly ground black pepper
to taste

Salad
2 tomatoes, cored and sliced
1 English cucumber, sliced
¼ lb (125 g) fresh buffalo mozzarella
(substitute kesong puti), sliced
Salt and freshly ground black pepper
to taste

Prepare the dressing: Combine the olive oil, *calamansi* juice, green onion (scallion), garlic, anchovy paste, fresh coriander leaves (cilantro), and sugar in a blender. Blend until smooth and season with salt and pepper. Pour the dressing into a small bowl and set aside.

Assemble the salad: Arrange alternating slices of tomato, cucumber, and mozzarella on a large serving platter. Spoon the dressing over the salad. Season with salt and pepper. Serve immediately.

One food you're sure to find in ample abundance across the islands from modest food stalls to upscale restaurants is *pusit*, or squid. Filipino homage to squid includes enjoying it dried, grilled, stewed in *adobo*, stuffed, even raw in *kilaw*. This grilled squid salad is an offshoot of a delicious dish my mother used to make of marinated squid tinged with vinegar, garlic, and onions. *Bagoong hipon*, or shrimp paste, was often on the table but I prefer adding it directly to the vinaigrette. If you're not comfortable cooking squid, now's the time to jump right in and see how easy it is. As a general rule, squid remains tender with quick, high-heat cooking (grilling, sautéing, or stir-frying for less than 5 minutes) or long, slow, moderate-heat cooking (stewing or braising for at least 25 minutes). We're taking the shorter route in this recipe.

Serves 4

Vinaigrette

2 tablespoons coconut or palm vinegar
1 clove garlic, peeled
1 teaspoon peeled and minced fresh ginger
1 teaspoon sugar
1 teaspoon shrimp paste
1 teaspoon fish sauce
Dash of dried red pepper flakes or ground red pepper
¼ cup (50 ml) olive oil

Salad

1 lb (450 g) whole baby squid, cleaned
2 tablespoons soy sauce
1 tablespoon olive oil
¼ teaspoon freshly ground black pepper
2 oz (50 g) cured Spanish chorizo, sliced
¼ cup (50 ml) pitted green Spanish olives
1 green onion (scallion), chopped
1 medium tomato, deseeded and diced
1 tablespoon chopped fresh coriander leaves (cilantro)

Make the vinaigrette: Combine the vinegar, garlic, ginger, sugar, shrimp paste, fish sauce, and dried red pepper flakes in a blender or food processor. While the machine is running, slowly drizzle in the olive oil. Set aside.

Marinate the squid: Place the squid, soy sauce, olive oil, and pepper in a bowl. Stir to combine and marinate for 5 minutes. Preheat the grill over a medium-high flame.

Cook the squid and assemble the salad: Grill the squid for 2 to 3 minutes per side until cooked through and place in a serving bowl. Add the chorizo, olives, green onion (scallion), tomato, and fresh coriander leaves (cilantro). Toss with the vinaigrette. Serve warm or chilled.

How to Clean Squid

Let's assume that you've decided to really get your hands dirty with squid and have admirably bypassed the dozens of varieties of precleaned, frozen squid. You've sniffed, picked, and prodded through the fishmonger's squid supply and chosen the best of the bunch. How do you transform the alienlike creatures into a sleek, white, ready-to-cook delicacy? You'll first want to pull out the "pen," the transparent, plasticlike shell of the squid attached to the inside body. It is easy to locate if you run your finger along the open edge of the body, just below the head. Next, separate the head from the body, also called the mantle. Hold the body firmly with one hand and the head with the other and pull the two apart. The innards should come trailing out loosely attached to the head. Separate the head from the tentacles by cutting above the eyes. Feel around the center base of the tentacles for the hard bonelike "beak." Remove and discard that along with the head and innards. Set the tentacles aside. Starting at the wings attached to the base of the squid body, peel off and discard the mantle's purple skin, revealing opaque white flesh. The tentacles and body are now ready to use.

WATER SPINACH SALAD WITH SESAME DRESSING

Water spinach and bean sprouts combined in salad may seem like an odd couple. But once you get past the slippery *kangkong* leaves, which don't play much part in this dish, you get to the kangkong stems, which have the same addictive quality that bean sprouts boast—an irresistible crispness that makes for a snappy toothy salad. The bean sprouts should be firm and fresh when you purchase them and used immediately. Trim the kangkong leaves from the hollow stems and reserve them for Adobong Kangkong (page 138), or as a spinach substitute. This recipe for spicy sesame dressing will leave you with enough leftover to drizzle on grilled vegetables or a green salad.

Makes 4 servings

Sesame Dressing: makes ½ cup (125 ml)

¼ cup (50 ml) olive oil
1 tablespoon sesame oil
1 tablespoon palm or coconut vinegar
2 to 3 calamansi, zest and juice (substitute lime, 1 tablespoon each of zest and juice)
1 teaspoon shrimp paste
2 teaspoons fish sauce
1 teaspoon peeled and chopped fresh ginger
2 teaspoons granulated sugar
½ teaspoon sambal ulek or dried red pepper flakes

Salad

6 cups (1½ liters) water
½ lb (225 g) bean sprouts
¼ lb (125 g) kangkong stems, washed and sliced into pieces
1 green onion (scallion), finely chopped
Salt and ground pepper to taste
2 tablespoons crushed roasted peanuts

Make the dressing: Combine the olive oil, sesame oil, vinegar, citrus zest and juice, shrimp paste, fish sauce, ginger, sugar, and sambal ulek in a blender. Blend on high until smooth. Pour the dressing into a small bowl and set aside. Store in an airtight container in the refrigerator for up to 2 weeks.

Make the salad: Boil the water in a medium pot over high heat. Add the bean sprouts to pot and blanch for 1 minute. Use a mesh strainer to remove the sprouts from the water into a colander. Plunge the sprouts into a bowl of ice water to immediately stop the cooking. Drain the sprouts well and pat dry with paper towels. Place in a large bowl. Return the pot of water to a boil. Add the kangkong stems and cook for 3 to 4 minutes until tender but still crispy. Remove the stems from the pot and shock in ice water as you did with the bean sprouts. Drain well, pat dry with paper towels, and add to the bean sprouts. Add the green onion (scallion) and ¼ cup (50 ml) of the sesame dressing. Toss to combine. Season with salt and pepper. Sprinkle with crushed peanuts before serving.

PALM HEARTS AND APPLE SALAD WITH CALAMANSI MAYONNAISE

Ubod, or young coconut palm hearts, are a delicacy in Filipino cuisine, particularly enjoyed in fresh *lumpia ubod* spring rolls or pickled in achara. The potent combination of tart apple, herbaceous celery, and creamy palm hearts forms a refreshing trio that will make this salad a regular addition to your repertoire.

Serves 4

Calamansi Mayonnaise: makes 1 cup (250 ml)
1 large egg yolk
3 tablespoons calamansi juice
1 tablespoon honey
1 teaspoon mustard
1½ teaspoons peeled and finely minced fresh ginger
1 teaspoon salt
Dash of freshly ground black pepper
1 cup (250 ml) vegetable oil

Salad
8 oz (225 g) hearts of palm, sliced
1 Granny Smith apple, peeled, cored, and cut into ⅛-in (3-mm) matchsticks
Two 2-in (5-cm) pieces celery, cut into thin matchsticks
1 shallot, very thinly sliced
¼ cup (25 g) chopped roasted cashews
Dash of sea salt

Make the mayonnaise: Place the egg yolk, calamansi juice, honey, mustard, ginger, salt, and pepper in a food processor and start the machine. As the machine is running, very slowly add the oil in a thin stream through the top feed. If you add the oil too quickly, it will not emulsify with the egg. Check the consistency of the mayonnaise. If it is too thick, add a few drops of water. If it is too thin, continue to add up to ¼ cup (50 ml) more oil until it reaches your desired thickness.

Scoop the mayonnaise into an airtight container and keep in the refrigerator until ready to use.

Make the salad: Combine the palm hearts, apple, celery, shallot, and ½ cup (125 ml) of the mayonnaise in a bowl. Toss to combine and chill for 30 minutes. Sprinkle the salad with the chopped cashews and sea salt before serving.

MARINATED SALMON SALAD WITH FENNEL SALMON KILAW

Kilaw is both a cooking technique as well as a specific dish. Lightly marinating fish in an acid such as lime juice, vinegar, or tamarind is a wonderful method of "cooking" fish so that it retains its freshness and texture. I particularly like using heavily flavored fish such as salmon, mackerel, or sardines for this recipe because their dominant flavors not only couple well with the five-spice vinegar but complement the anise-flavored fennel.

Serves 4

½ lb (225 g) fresh salmon fillet
1¼ cups (300 ml) Five-Spice Vinegar
   (see page 18)
3 tablespoons Coconut Cream (see
   page 16)
¼ teaspoon salt
Dash of freshly ground black pepper
1 small fennel bulb, thinly shaved
2 cups (50 g) baby salad greens
2 lime wedges
Sea salt

Marinate the salmon: Place the salmon fillet in a nonreactive dish. Pour 1 cup (250 ml) of the five-spice vinegar over the salmon and cover with plastic wrap. Marinate for 15 minutes in the refrigerator. Turn the fillet over and marinate another 15 minutes. The flesh will turn an opaque pink but the center of the fillet will remain translucent. Remove the fillet from the dish and discard the marinade. Slice the salmon into ¼-inch (6-mm) slices. Set aside.

Make the salad dressing: Combine the remaining ¼ cup (50 ml) five-spice vinegar with the coconut cream, salt, and pepper. Whisk the ingredients together.

Make the fennel salad: In another bowl combine the shaved fennel and salad greens. Pour the coconut dressing over the salad and lightly toss. Arrange the salad on a serving platter. Lay the sliced salmon around the salad. Squeeze the salmon lightly with lime and sprinkle with sea salt just before serving.

BLACK AND WHITE RICE WITH SEAFOOD PAELLA PIRURUTONG A LA FILIPINA

GARLIC FRIED RICE SINANGAG

FRAGRANT RICE WITH GREEN MANGO SINANGAG NGA MAY MANGGA

PANCIT GUISADO

PANCIT PALABOK/PANCIT LUGLUG

PANCIT SOTANGHON WITH BEEF AND BROCCOLI

CUBAN-STYLE RICE ARROZ A LA CUBANA

COCONUT NOODLES WITH MUSHROOMS AND TOFU PANCIT BUTONG

SAFFRON RICE WITH CHINESE SAUSAGE

SPICY RICE WITH CHICKEN AND PEPPERS BRINGHE

RICE AND NOODLE DISHES

For centuries throughout the Philippines one crop has remained the most consequential in sustaining life, providing millions of Filipinos their most common and basic food—rice. It is the main food eaten at least three times a day with accompanying dishes such as fish, meats, soups, and vegetables playing supporting roles as condiments. With rice so intricately woven into the fabric of Filipino life, how do the dietary necessities of a predominantly rural developing country like the Philippines translate on American soil where a low-carb, high-protein, meat-focused regimen is becoming the dietary standard?

The answer lies on the table. Necessity once dictated that rice held its dominant position at the center of the table around which small offerings of meat, fish, soups, or vegetables were placed as "seasonings." For many Filipinos, beef, pork, and poultry are not necessarily everyday fare but special occasion indulgences reserved for holidays, fiestas, and patron saint celebrations. However, because America's land is that of immeasurable bounty providing a seemingly endless variety of accessible, affordable, and convenient protein sources that perhaps are unavailable in the homeland, necessity can quietly (and I'm sure happily) take a backseat to tradition. Steamed white rice is certainly still served at every Filipino meal, even if Filipino fare is not being served. But for many Filipino-Americans, the Occidental dinner template of protein, vegetable, and starch applies. Rice has a permanently reserved spot on the table, but as an accompaniment to the entrée instead of as the main course.

There are literally thousands of varieties of rice. Filipinos are partial to long-grain indica rice as their everyday rice, it being the variety predominantly grown in the fields of the Philippines. These would include traditional varieties such as *milagrosa* and *wagwag*, as well as high-yielding modern varieties called IR–64 and IR–36. Thai Jasmine rice, another popular variety, is a long-grain rice that has a floral aroma and cooks to a soft chewy texture that, unlike many long-grain varieties, retains a slight stickiness that Asians love in their rice. Medium-grain calrose rice is also an excellent table rice in that it cooks plump, fluffy, and sticky. Pilafs don't usually find a place on the Filipino table and instant rice is rarely a welcomed guest in a Filipino house.

Everyday rice is simple—steamed or boiled without coloring or flavoring. Since plain rice accompanies most meals, you'll find a recipe for it in the "Basics" chapter. Some subtle flavor variations on steamed rice are included in this chapter and certainly worth trying, especially since it requires the addition of only one, or perhaps two ingredients. Garlicky Sinangag, heady, aromatic, and addictive as popcorn, is often combined with other foods to make a complete meal. Fried rice is best made with day-old rice (long-grain Jasmine or Milagrosa rice works marvelously) that has lost its freshly cooked stickiness. I have also included a couple of recipes using short-grain, sweet (also called glutinous) rice that we call *malagkit*. Malagkit has a sticky texture similar to Italian risotto that makes delectable steamed desserts, although it is equally versatile in the savory rice dishes flavored with meats and seafood that I've featured here.

Noodles are another Filipino staple, although they are not burdened with the responsibility that rice carries in completing a meal. Generally termed *pancit*, noodles came into the Philippines as they did in the rest of the world, by way of the Chinese. *Panciterias* usually refer to Chinese restaurants that not only serve a variety of pancit but Chinese specialties as well. Pancit dishes are easily distinguished by the type of noodle used, a distinction made by attaching the noodle variety after the word pancit as demonstrated in the recipe titles. And what a variety of noodles there are! Noodle choices may include *miki, mami, bihon, luglug, sotanghon, Canton*, and more. A helpful noodle guide is listed in "The Grocery Store" so that you can confidently navigate through the sea of choices. The cooking technique behind pancit is roughly the same in each recipe, so do try several recipes. Certain noodles and flavorings make significant differences in the dish, making each pancit entirely unique.

BLACK AND WHITE RICE WITH SEAFOOD PAELLA PIRURUTONG A LA FILIPINA

This dish is hardly a traditional paella, by any Spanish standard. In fact, any self-respecting Spanish cook would no doubt frown at the elements that stray from the motherland favorite: black rice (*pirurutong*), precooked white rice, fish sauce, coconut milk, *no saffron!* This *arroz* doesn't strive to be paella in any respect other than in the cooking method, which so differs from the plain steamed rice characteristic of the Islands. Imbued with Filipino flavors and piled high with succulent seafood, this paella-style dish is irrefutably delicious and rewarding. Using day-old cooked rice may seem like a shortcut to the traditional paella-method of sautéing raw rice in oil and cooking it slowly in broth with meats or seafood. However, as with many foreign dishes introduced by the Spaniards, Filipinos have tweaked traditional recipes to suit their resources and palates. The texture of fully cooked steamed rice is preferable to the European al dente standard. Because this recipe calls for day-old cooked rice, this paella is actually quick enough to make during the week for an impressive and satisfying one-pan meal.

Serves 6

2 tablespoons olive oil

6 to 8 large sea scallops (approximately ¼ lb/125 g)

½ lb (225 g) shrimp, peeled and deveined

¼ lb (125 g) squid, cleaned (see page 68), and sliced into rings

1 yellow onion, diced

2 cloves garlic, chopped

1 cup (200 g) cherry or grape tomatoes, halved

¼ lb (125 g) chorizo de Bilbao, sliced

4 cups (725 g) cooked day-old long-grain rice (see Steamed Rice recipe, page 21)

1 cup (200 g) cooked black rice (use Thai black sticky rice or Chinese forbidden black rice; follow cooking directions on package)

1 cup (125 g) frozen or fresh peas

2 cups (500 ml) Shrimp or Fish Stock (see page 14)

½ cup (125 ml) coconut milk

2 tablespoons fish sauce

½ teaspoon freshly ground black pepper

1 lb (450 g) black mussels, cleaned

Heat the oil in a 12 to14-inch (30 to 35-cm) paella pan or sauté pan over medium-high heat. When the oil is hot add the scallops to the pan. Sear each side for 2 to 3 minutes, until well browned. Remove from the pan to a plate. Add the shrimp to the pan; cook and stir for 3 to 4 minutes until opaque orange and nearly cooked through. Remove to the same plate as the scallops and set aside. Add the squid to the pan and cook for 2 to 3 minutes until opaque. Set aside on the same plate with the scallops and shrimp.

Stir the onion, garlic, and tomatoes into the pan. Cook for 1 minute until the onion is translucent. Add the chorizo de Bilbao to the pan; cook and stir for 2 minutes. Add the cooked white rice, cooked black rice, peas, shrimp stock, coconut milk, fish sauce, and pepper to the pan. Stir together. Return the scallops, shrimp, and squid to the pan. Arrange the mussels over the rice and loosely cover the pan with a fitted cover or aluminum foil, allowing the steam to escape. Simmer 5 to 6 minutes until the mussels open and the rice absorbs much of the liquid. The rice will appear wet but will continue to absorb liquid as it cools. Serve immediately.

GARLIC FRIED RICE SINANGAG

Not to be confused with *sinigang*, or sour soup (page 48), *sinangag* (shown opposite) is a simple yet satisfying garlic fried rice. Often served as a breakfast staple, sinangag makes good use of day-old rice that is past its prime having lost its fresh-cooked stickiness. When marinated meat (*tapa*) is paired with sinangag and a sunny-side up egg (*itlog*), the trio is a classic breakfast combination that has morphed into *tapsilog* in Filipino vernacular. *Longsilog* replaces *tapa* with *longaniza* (sausage). *Tocilog* uses *tocino* (sweetened pork) and *bangsilog*, *bangus* (milkfish). Then there are the American flavors of *baconsilog* and *cornedbeefsilog*, inevitable additions to the Filipino-American breakfast. This sinangag recipe embraces the basic flavors of garlic and rice without distraction from common additions of soy sauce, fish sauce, ginger, scallions, or shallots. Using long-grain rice is an important factor in achieving a fried rice that is perfectly fluffy and separated. Medium and short-grain rice tends to be moist, even after a day or two, which leads to sticky clumps of fried rice.

Serves 4

2 tablespoons olive oil
2 small cloves garlic, chopped
4 cups (725 ml) cooked day-old long-grain rice (see Steamed Rice recipe, page 21)
½ teaspoon salt
¼ teaspoon freshly ground black pepper

Heat the olive oil in a 10 to 12-inch (25 to 30-cm) nonstick skillet or wok over medium-low heat. Add the garlic, cooking and stirring until lightly toasted to a golden brown. Add the rice and cook for 5 minutes, stirring occasionally, until each grain is heated through and lightly fried. Season with salt and pepper. Ladle the rice onto a platter and serve hot.

Variation: Salmon and Garlic Fried Rice. Leftover salmon makes a terrific addition to the classic garlic fried rice. If you're using canned salmon, completely drain any canning liquid before using. After toasting the garlic in the oil, add 1½ cups (175 g) cooked flaked salmon to the skillet and sauté for 1 minute. Add the rice and cook until warmed through and lightly fried. Season with salt and pepper.

FRAGRANT RICE WITH GREEN MANGO SINANGAG NGA MAY MANGGA

The Filipino palate is not shy when it comes to strong flavors, and often rice is the perfect neutral backdrop with which to enjoy more assertive native ingredients. Pungent shrimp paste and tart green mango, for example, are duly revered in their respective roles as seasonings for other dishes but also enjoyed paired together as a common snack. Add fried rice and toasted garlic to the mix and plain *sinangag* gets a dramatic makeover. Fresh chives are my herb of choice, providing just a hint of flavor. But feel free to go for the gusto with more fragrant herbs such as fresh coriander leaves (cilantro), mint, oregano, or basil. (See photograph, page 21.)

Serves 4

3 tablespoons olive oil
1 teaspoon sesame oil
1 clove garlic, chopped
2 green onions (scallions), finely chopped
1 cup (175 g) peeled green mango, cut into ½-in (1½-cm) cubes

1 teaspoon shrimp paste
4 cups (725 g) cooked day-old long-grain rice (see Steamed Rice recipe, page 21)
¼ cup (10 g) chopped chives

Heat the olive oil and sesame oil together in a 10-inch (25-cm) sauté pan over medium-high heat.

Add the garlic, green onions (scallions), and green mango; cook and stir for 2 minutes until the garlic is lightly toasted. Add the shrimp paste and cook another 30 seconds. Add the rice and sauté for 5 to 6 minutes until heated through and well mixed with the seasonings. Stir in the chives and spoon onto a serving platter.

PANCIT GUISADO

The Chinese are largely responsible for the wide range of Filipino noodle dishes that are collectively termed *pancit*. A national staple offered in the most modest food stall to the refined dine-in establishment, pancit dishes are almost as essential as rice. Often distinguished by the type of noodle used, *pancit bihon* (rice stick noodles), *pancit miki* (thin, round egg noodles), *pancit sotanghon* (mung bean thread noodles), or *pancit mami* (flat, wide egg noodles) are among the many dishes that Filipinos have imbued with their own style and flavor. *Guisado* means "stewed"—a sort of catchall term for pancits that don't fit into any of the classic categories. It's an apt name for this pancit recipe since we're using a combination of mung bean thread noodles and fresh, egg noodles that resemble homemade angel hair pasta but without the semolina. Dried Canton noodles are a fine backup although the flavor and texture of the noodles will differ slightly. Don't be alarmed by the number of ingredients in this and other pancit recipes, which may seem a little daunting, especially with all of the slicing, dicing, and shredding inevitably required. Once you've gathered and prepared your ingredients, the actual cooking time is very short.

Serves 6

3 to 4 dried shiitake mushrooms
½ cup (125 ml) rice wine
½ cup (125 ml) hot water
2 oz (50 g) dried mung bean thread noodles, approximately 2 bundles
2 tablespoons olive oil
1 small onion, diced
2 cloves garlic, chopped
½ teaspoon peeled and minced fresh ginger
¼ lb (125 g) Chinese sausage or chorizo de Bilbao, diced
¼ lb (125 g) chicken breast, diced
3 teaspoons soy sauce
2 tablespoons oyster sauce
2 cups (500 ml) Chicken Stock (see page 15)
¼ teaspoon freshly ground black pepper
8 oz (225 g) fresh thin, round egg noodles
1 carrot, peeled and cut into matchsticks
1 stalk celery, thinly sliced
2 cups (175 g) finely shredded Napa cabbage
1 green onion (scallion), sliced

Place dried shiitake mushrooms in a bowl with rice wine and hot water. Soak mushrooms 15 to 20 minutes until softened. Remove mushrooms from bowl, reserving the soaking liquid. Remove and discard woody stems and slice mushroom caps thinly. Set aside.

Soak mung bean thread noodles in warm water for 5 minutes until softened. Drain water and set noodles aside.

Heat olive oil in a large skillet over medium heat. Sauté onion, garlic, and ginger for 1 minute, making sure that the garlic does not burn. Add sausage and chicken. Continue sautéing another 4 to 5 minutes, until chicken turns opaque. Add soy, oyster sauce, chicken stock, reconstituted mushrooms, mushroom soaking liquid, and black pepper. Reduce heat to a low simmer for 5 minutes until chicken is cooked through. Add the egg noodles and bean thread noodles, making sure that they are completely submerged in the cooking liquid. Simmer 5 to 7 minutes until noodles are tender. Add carrots, celery, and Napa cabbage. Toss all ingredients together so that they are well combined. Garnish with sliced green onion (scallion).

PANCIT PALABOK/PANCIT LUGLUG

Palabok is distinguished from other *pancit* by the orange-tinged sauce and the impressive array of garnishes used to season and adorn the noodles. Toasted garlic, pork crackling, smoked fish flakes (*tinapa*), and hard-boiled eggs are among the signature toppings that lend high-impact flavor and texture to this dish. The eye-catching, rust-colored sauce is a tantalizing shrimp sauce made from *annatto*-infused shrimp juice. *Bihon* noodles (also called rice stick noodles) are the canvas underlying the colorful palabok sauce. Made from either cornstarch or a blend of cornstarch and rice flour, bihon are round angel hair noodles that have something of a slippery texture, which splendidly offsets the meaty trimmings.

Admittedly, in this recipe the ingredients list is unique and the procedural steps are more than a few. But you'll save valuable time in assembling the dish by purchasing a good quality shrimp or fish stock for your sauce and having your garnishes prepared in advance.

Pancit Luglug is *palabok's* fraternal twin, sharing the same sauce and garnishes. The difference lies in the noodle. *Luglug* also uses a cornstarch noodle but one that is thicker than bihon.

Serves 4

Sauce

1 lb (450 g) shell-on shrimp
1 tablespoon annatto seeds
2½ cups (625 ml) shrimp juice or Shrimp Stock (see page 14)
3 tablespoons all-purpose flour
1 tablespoon soy sauce
1 tablespoon fish sauce
¼ teaspoon freshly ground black pepper
8 oz (225 g) dried bihon, cornstarch stick noodles
¼ cup (10 g) chopped fresh corriander leaves (cilantro)

Topping

1 lb (450 g) cooked peeled shrimp, from palabok sauce
¼ lb (125 g) diced chicharon, pork crackling
¼ cup (50 g) flaked tinapa, smoked fish
1 tablespoon Toasted Garlic (see page 17)
2 hard-boiled eggs, sliced into rounds
4 to 5 calamansi, halved (substitute 1 lime, sliced into wedges)

Make the shrimp juice: Place the shrimp in a single layer on a baking sheet and broil for 10 to 12 minutes, turning the shrimp over halfway through cooking. Cool the shrimp to the touch and peel. Reserve the cooked shrimp for the topping. Place the shells in a food processor with the annatto seeds and 2 cups (500 ml) water; process until finely mashed. Pour the shell mixture into a fine strainer and press to extract the shrimp juice. Discard the shells and seeds. If you are using premade shrimp stock instead of shrimp shells, soak the annatto seeds in 2 cups (500 ml) shrimp broth for 30 minutes to infuse the color and flavor. Strain and reserve the broth, discarding the seeds.

Make the sauce: Pour 2 cups shrimp juice into a large sauté pan (3 to 4 quart/liter) and simmer over low heat. Mix together the remaining ½ cup (125 ml) juice (or stock) in a cup with the flour, soy sauce, fish sauce, and pepper, stirring until smooth. Add the flour mixture to the pan and stir to combine. Simmer for 5 minutes until thickened. Set aside but keep warm.

Prepare the noodles: For Pancit Palabok, use bihon noodles; for Pancit Luglug, use luglug noodles. Bring a pot of water to a boil. Add the noodles to the pot, swirling them so that they do not stick together. After 2 to 3 minutes, taste a noodle for doneness; it should be tender but not mushy. Drain the noodles and place in a serving dish. Pour the sauce over the noodles and sprinkle with the chopped cilantro; toss well to combine.

Prepare the tinapa: Simply panfry the tinapa whole in a scant tablespoon of oil until cooked through or place the fish under the broiler for 7 to 8 minutes per side. You can also cook the fish by poaching it in water to remove a little of the salt and smokiness that some might find overpowering. Flake the fillets from the bones for use on your pancit.

Garnish the pancit: Arrange the shrimp over the noodles. Sprinkle the pork crackling, flaked tinapa, and toasted garlic evenly over the noodles. Lay the slices of egg around the edges of the serving dish. Serve with halved calamansi or wedges of lime.

A Note on Substitutions

The garnishes used in this recipe are only a few of the traditional toppings suggested for *pancit palabok*. If you have trouble finding *tinapa* or fresh *chicharon*, don't feel like your pancit will be in any way compromised. Simply omit the ingredients you don't have and use comparable substitutes. Cooked sliced pork, sautéed Chinese sausage, or prepackaged pork sung (cooked, dried, shredded pork) are fine replacements for chicharon, and dried bonito flakes or dried shrimp and a sprinkle of smoked paprika are excellent substitutes for tinapa. Sliced green onions (scallions), roasted peanuts, fried tofu, and *kinchay* (Chinese celery) are also fair game when decorating your pancit palabok.

PANCIT SOTANGHON WITH BEEF AND BROCCOLI

Of the dozens of noodles on the market, bean thread noodles, or *sotanghon*, are one of my favorites. They're incredibly versatile, appearing in soups, stuffed in a spring roll, stewed in a *pancit* with meats or vegetables, quickly stir-fried, even deep-fried as a crispy garnish. Made from the starch of mung beans, these quick-cooking cellophane noodles (also called bean thread vermicelli) can be cooked directly in your pot of broth, an important feature when fast meals are as much a priority as healthy delicious ones. To speed their cooking time even more, and to make them easier to handle, I soften the noodles in a bowl of hot water for five minutes. The rest of your ingredients should be nearly cooked by the time you add your noodles since, once softened, they need only a couple of minutes to reach full doneness.

Serves 4

7 oz (200 g), approximately 4 bundles, dried mung bean thread noodles

4 cups (1 liter) hot tap water

1 tablespoon olive oil

1 small onion, diced

2 cloves garlic, chopped

1 teaspoon peeled and minced fresh ginger

¾ lb (350 g) beef sirloin, thinly sliced

¼ cup (50 ml) rice wine

1 tablespoon fish sauce

1 tablespoon soy sauce

1 teaspoon sambal ulek or dried red pepper flakes

2 cups (500 ml) Beef Stock (see page 14)

½ lb (225 g) broccoli florets

1 green onion (scallion), chopped

Place the bean thread noodles in a large bowl and cover with hot water for 5 minutes until the noodles are soft. Drain the water and set the noodles aside. Often the noodle bundles are tied with a barely noticeable piece of white string. Be sure to remove that string before soaking the noodles.

Heat the olive oil in a large (3 to 4-quart/liter) skillet or wok over medium-high heat. When the oil is hot but not smoking, add the onion, garlic, and ginger. Stir-fry for 30 seconds being careful not to burn the garlic. Add the beef to the pan and stir-fry for another 2 minutes.

Deglaze the pan with the rice wine. Season with the fish sauce, soy sauce, sambal ulek, and beef stock. Bring the broth to a simmer. Add the broccoli and cover. Simmer for 5 minutes until the broccoli is almost tender. Remove the cover and add the noodles to the pan so that they are completely submerged in the broth. Cook the noodles for another 3 to 4 minutes, mixing them well into the broth. Remove from the heat and garnish with the chopped green onion (scallion).

CUBAN-STYLE RICE ARROZ A LA CUBANA

Depending on whom you ask, the daily restaurant ritual of serving a family-style meal to the staff may be considered either an occupational benefit or bane. I've always considered the staff meal an essential component of operations, offering the staff nourishment and respite before the nonstop hustle of dinner service. But it often poses challenges for the line cooks who are faced with what to make in the least amount of time using inexpensive ingredients. Hmm, sound familiar? It's America's nightly dinner dilemma. This addictive rice dish was an easy answer—quick, cheap, and a convenient way to use rice, meat, and vegetable leftovers. Ground beef or pork makes a fresh *picadillo* but I've made this *arroz* using leftover shredded pork with mouthwatering results. Sweet plantains and fried eggs are the signature toppers that make it undeniably satisfying.

Serves 4

6 tablespoons oil
1 large ripe plantain (approximately 10 oz/280 g), peeled and sliced into ½-in (1⅓-cm)-thick rounds
1 small onion, chopped
2 cloves garlic, chopped
1 small tomato, diced
1 lb (450 g) ground beef or pork
¼ teaspoon ground cinnamon
¼ teaspoon dried oregano
¼ cup (50 g) chopped green olives
1½ teaspoons soy sauce
½ cup (125 ml) Chicken Stock (see page 15)
1 potato, cut into ½-in (1⅓-cm) cubes
8 oz (225 g) frozen or fresh peas
3 cups (550 g) cooked long-grain white rice (see page 21)
4 eggs, cooked over easy

Heat 5 tablespoons of the oil in a medium skillet over medium heat. Fry the plantain in the hot oil or 3 to 4 minutes per side until the plantain becomes golden brown. Dry on paper towels. Set aside.

Add the remaining tablespoon oil to the skillet and sauté the onion, garlic, and tomato for 2 minutes until tomato becomes tender. Add the ground meat and cook for 7 to 9 minutes to render off the fat. Pour off the excess fat into a bowl and discard.

Add the cinnamon, oregano, olives, soy sauce, and chicken stock. Reduce the heat to a low simmer. Add the potato and peas. Cook for 8 to10 minutes until the meat is fully cooked and the potato is tender. Stir in rice and cook until warmed through. Spoon the rice mixture on a plate and serve with plantain rounds and over-easy eggs.

COCONUT NOODLES WITH MUSHROOMS AND TOFU
PANCIT BUTONG

With faux noodles fashioned from tender slices of young coconut meat, *pancit butong* may seem like a contrived restaurant concoction instead of a native Filipino specialty. It is, in fact, a traditional pancit that just so happens to deviate from the standard template. Starch-based noodles and meats are replaced by coconut noodles and tofu for a vegetarian pancit that is characteristically Filipino and deliciously unique. Thinly shaved *buko*, or young coconut meat, is the secret to the "noodle." You'll find buko canned in tender chunks that are easily cut into matchsticks or shaved with a peeler for paper-thin slices. For easy convenience, buko also comes pre-cut in frozen blocks. A roasted mushroom medley of your favorite wild mushrooms is the vegetable paradigm for robust flavor and soulful satisfaction. Toasted garlic (page 17) sprinkled atop the dish is guaranteed to lend its alluring aroma and unapologetic flavor.

Serves 4

Roasted Mushrooms
½ lb (225 g) assorted mush-
    rooms (oyster, shiitake,
    chanterelle, or enoki)
3 tablespoons melted butter
Salt and freshly ground black pepper
    to taste

Pancit
2 tablespoons olive oil
4 oz (125 g) extra-firm tofu, diced
    into ½-in (1⅓-cm) cubes
1 green onion (scallion), sliced
1 red Thai chile, chopped
¼ cup (50 ml) rice wine
¼ cup (50 ml) Vegetable Stock (see
    page 15)
2 tablespoons mushroom soy sauce
3 cups (675 ml) young coconut
    meat cut into matchsticks
1 teaspoon chopped oregano
3 *calamansi,* halved

Roast the mushrooms: Position the oven rack within 6 to 8 inches (15 to 20 cm) of the broiler. Arrange the mushrooms on a sheet pan lined with parchment paper or aluminum foil. Pour the melted butter over the mushrooms and season with salt and pepper. Broil the mushrooms for 10 to 15 minutes, stirring occasionally to evenly roast the mushrooms. They should be tender and nicely browned. Remove the mushrooms from the oven and set aside.

Make the pancit: Heat the olive oil in a medium sauté pan over medium-high heat. When the oil is hot, add the diced tofu and brown on all sides. Add the green onion (scallion) and chile and cook for 30 seconds. Deglaze the pan with the rice wine. Add the vegetable stock, mushroom soy sauce, coconut meat, and roasted mushrooms. Cover and simmer for 3 to 5 minutes until heated through. Remove the cover and stir in the oregano. Spoon the pancit into bowls and garnish with the *calamansi.*

SAFFRON RICE WITH CHINESE SAUSAGE

The flavors of two continents converge in this simple yet satisfying dish with Spanish saffron and Chinese sausage (shown opposite). As the superstar of the spice world, saffron earns its reputation by imparting its honey gold color and alluring flavor with just a few precious strands. Paired with Chinese *lop chong*, with its compelling mixture of smoke, spice, and sweetness, the collaboration of ingredients is truly rewarding.

Serves 4

1 teaspoon olive oil
2 cloves garlic, minced
1 shallot, chopped
4 oz (125 g) Chinese sausage, sliced
3 to 4 saffron strands
2 cups (500 ml) Chicken Stock (see page 15)
1 tablespoon soy sauce

Dash of freshly ground black pepper
1 cup (200 g) uncooked jasmine rice or any long-grain rice

Heat the olive oil in a medium pot (2 to 3 quarts/liters) over medium heat. Add the garlic, shallot, and Chinese sausage. Cook and stir for 1 minute, being careful not to burn the garlic. Add the saffron, chicken broth, soy sauce, and pepper. Simmer for 5 minutes.

Add the rice and stir to combine. Cover the pot and reduce the heat to the lowest setting. Steam the rice for 20 to 25 minutes until tender.

SPICY RICE WITH CHICKEN AND PEPPERS BRINGHE

Bringhe is the classic combination of chicken and rice made special by a persuasive seasoning paste that infuses each grain of rice with the vivid flavors of ginger, yellow curry, and chiles. Glutinous rice, or *malagkit*, teams up with coconut milk for a smooth creamy dish that is reminiscent of Italian risotto but with all the flavors of Southeast Asia. If you've never worked with glutinous rice, any mystery it holds is easily overcome. It is cooked in a 1½-to-1 liquid-to-rice ratio and when cooked is delicately sticky. Although it's not necessary, I suggest soaking the grains in water for at least one hour to promote faster, even cooking.

Serves 4

Seasoning Paste
1 clove garlic, peeled
1 teaspoon peeled and chopped fresh ginger
1 green onion (scallion), chopped
1 small green or red Thai chile (*sili labuyo*), stem removed
1 teaspoon yellow curry powder
1 teaspoon shrimp paste (*bagoong alamang*)
1 teaspoon fish sauce
1 teaspoon granulated sugar
2 tablespoons olive oil

Rice
1 tablespoon olive oil
1 lb (450 g) skinless chicken breast, cut into ½-in (13-mm) cubes

2 cups (400 g) uncooked glutinous rice (*malagkit*), soaked in 4 cups (1 liter) water for 1 hour and drained
2 cups (500 ml) Chicken Stock (see page 15)
1 cup (250 ml) coconut milk
1 large banana leaf, rinsed and cut to fit your skillet or sauté pan
1 red bell pepper, deseeded and cut into 1-in (2½-cm) cubes

Make the seasoning paste: Combine the garlic, ginger, green onion (scallion), chile, curry powder, shrimp paste, fish sauce, sugar, and olive oil in a blender or food processor. Blend until well mashed into a paste. Set aside.

Make the rice: Heat the olive oil over medium heat in a large (3 to 4-quart/liter) skillet or sauté pan. When the oil is hot but not smoking, add the seasoning paste. Cook and stir for 1 minute. Add the chicken and cook for 5 minutes. Add the rice, chicken broth, and coconut milk. Stir to blend well. Lower the heat and set the banana leaf on top of the rice. Place a cover over the skillet and simmer the rice for 15 minutes. Remove the cover and banana leaf and add the bell pepper to the rice. Return the banana leaf and cover and simmer for another 10 to 15 minutes until the rice is tender and the chicken is cooked through. Serve immediately.

CHICKEN POTPIE PASTEL NGA MANOK

CHICKEN IN PEANUT SAUCE PIPIÁN

FRIED CHICKEN PRITONG MANOK

CHICKEN STEW WITH ROASTED PEPPERS AND POTATOES APRITADA NGA MANOK

BRAISED TURKEY WITH STUFFING PAKSIW NGA PABO

DUCK ADOBO WITH PINEAPPLE AND DATES ADOBONG PATO A LA MONJA

CITRUS-GINGER CHICKEN INASAL MANOK

STUFFED QUAIL RELLENONG PUGO

POULTRY

For many Filipinos living on the islands, food comes from the bounty of one's own backyard. Gardens planted with eggplant, tomatoes, corn, green beans, and squash provide year-round crops that supply the family with sustenance at every meal. But a backyard bounty is not limited to what grows in the garden. It often includes what grazes in the yard. Chickens, called *manok*, are a common household flock often found roaming the grounds and noisily rousing the neighbors. In addition to homegrown birds, the commercial chicken industry is a thriving business providing Filipinos with an inexpensive alternative to more costly proteins such as beef or certain seafoods. Filipino cuisine firmly embraces chicken with a delicious array of soups, stews, barbecues, and roasts featuring this venerable bird.

Because commercially produced chicken is generally neutral in taste, Filipinos are partial to cooking chicken on the bone, which keeps the meat tender, moist, and ultimately more flavorful. While the ease and convenience of boneless chicken breast is the preferred standard in the United States, Filipinos favor the dark meat of thighs, wings, and legs which are more suited to the longer cooking times required for many Filipino dishes like Adobo, Paksiw, Apritada, or even a simple Inasal barbecue. Breast meat is typically sliced into small pieces and reserved for stir-fries or as a meat element in noodle and rice dishes.

Inasal Manok features the simplicity of roasted (or grilled) chicken made special with a tangy marinade of citrus and fish sauce. Pritong Manok, or fried chicken, is another example of how a pungent marinade can elevate the versatile flavor of chicken. Though typically made with legs wings or thighs, I've opted to use boneless chicken breast for a quick dish that can be served as a main course, as a kids meal sliced into chicken fingers, or as a hearty sandwich perfect for lunch or a picnic. Pastel nga Manok is your basic chicken potpie with a uniquely Filipino filling bubbling underneath flaky puff pastry. Pipían, which refers to the sauce more than the dish, is one of the Mexican treasures brought to the islands by the Spaniards. Although very different in flavor than the Mexican original, which uses pumpkin or sesame seeds to flavor the stew, the Filipino version is traditionally made with peanuts and thickened with toasted rice flour.

Because Filipino cuisine bursts with vibrant flavors, game birds, with their darker meat, integrate beautifully into our recipes. The signature *adobo manok*, or chicken adobo, is given a new twist with the use of duck that, with the simple addition of tomatoes and pineapple, recalls the traditional style of the nuns, or *Adobong Pato a la Monja*. Another signature dish, *rellenong manok*, an elaborately stuffed whole chicken, is replaced by the more manageable and more flavorful semiboneless quail, perfect for individual servings. Turkey, one of my favorite game birds, has always taken center stage at our Thanksgiving table. But the turkey leftover tradition was an equally anticipated event that filled our house with the mouthwatering aroma of *paksiw*, a bright stew of turkey, vinegar, and bay leaves. The recipe I've included here is not just reserved for the holidays but allows you to enjoy paksiw's complex flavors all year round.

CHICKEN POTPIE PASTEL NGA MANOK

Pastel looks just like a potpie on the outside. The main difference is a filling that is distinctly Filipino. Flavored with dried shiitake mushrooms, chorizo de Bilbao, and Edam cheese, this potpie is rich and complex like no other potpie. Filipino chorizo de Bilbao is slightly milder than Spanish chorizo and a little more difficult to find. So feel free to substitute a Spanish brand. The *pastel*, or pastry cover, can range in texture from a basic piecrust to a sturdy empanada dough or a delicate puff pastry, which I prefer for convenience sake.

Serves 4

2 to 3 dried shiitake mushrooms
1 cup (250 ml) hot water
2 tablespoons olive oil
1 small leek, finely chopped
1 teaspoon peeled and minced fresh
   ginger
2 tablespoons all-purpose flour
½ lb (225 g) chicken breast, diced
¼ lb (125 g) chorizo de Bilbao, sliced
1 cup (125 g) green peas
1 small carrot, diced
2 cups (500 ml) Chicken Stock (see
   page 15)
1 tablespoon soy sauce
¼ teaspoon freshly ground black
   pepper
1 cup (150 g) grated Edam cheese
   (substitute Gouda)
1 lb (450 g) store-bought puff pastry, thawed
1 large egg, beaten

Make the filling: Soak the dried shiitake mushrooms in hot water for 15 minutes until they soften. Remove the mushrooms from the water. Cut off and discard the woody stems. Slice the mushroom caps thinly and reserve with the soaking water.

Heat the olive oil in a large skillet over medium heat. Add the leek and ginger. Cook and stir for 2 minutes until the leek begins to wilt. Add the flour. Continue to cook and stir for 1 minute. Add the chicken, chorizo, peas, carrot, chicken stock, soy sauce, pepper, bay leaf, and the reserved mushrooms with the soaking water. Bring the mixture to a simmer for 15 to 20 minutes until the chicken is completely cooked and the sauce thickens. Stir in the cheese. Transfer the mixture to a round 2-quart/liter casserole dish.

Assemble and bake the pie: Preheat the oven to 375°F (190°C). Roll out the puff pastry at least 1 inch (2½ cm) larger than the size and shape of your casserole dish. Lay the dough over the casserole and fold the overhanging dough into a decorative edge. Use a knife to cut slits in the dough to allow steam to escape during cooking. Brush the dough with the beaten egg. Bake for 30 to 40 minutes until the dough puffs and turns a golden brown.

CHICKEN IN PEANUT SAUCE PIPIÁN

If you've ever enjoyed the pungent peanut sauce that regularly accompanies Southeast Asian *satay* (or *saté*), which is altogether zesty, spicy, and aromatic, then the familiar flavors of Filipino *pipían* are right up your alley. Chicken simmered in a complex peanut sauce tinged with the earthy color and flavor of *atsuete* (annatto) seeds and thickened with toasted rice flour makes for a deliciously different stew that needs nothing more than a large bowl of rice to sop up the abundant sauce. Add a steamed or sautéed vegetable to complete the meal.

Serves 4

1 tablespoon olive oil
1 teaspoon annatto seeds
2 lbs (900 g) chicken breast, skin removed
2 green onions (scallions), chopped
2 cloves garlic, minced
1 Thai small chile, chopped
1 tablespoon rice wine
2 teaspoons coconut vinegar
1 tablespoon rice flour
1½ cups (375 ml) Chicken Stock (see page 15)
2 tablespoons creamy peanut butter
1 tablespoon fish sauce
1 tablespoon chopped fresh coriander leaves (cilantro)
2 tablespoons coarsely ground roasted peanuts

Brown the chicken: Heat the olive oil in a large sauté pan (3 to 4 quarts/liters) over medium heat. Add the annatto seeds to the pan. Cook and stir for 4 to 5 minutes until the oil becomes rust-colored. Use a spoon to remove and discard the seeds. Increase the heat to medium-high. When the oil is smoking, add the chicken breast, being careful not to overcrowd the pan. Brown the chicken breast on both sides, 4 to 5 minutes per side. Remove the chicken from the pan and set on a plate.

Make the sauce: Add the green onions (scallions), garlic, and chile to the pan. Sauté for 1 minute, being careful not to burn the vegetables. Deglaze the pan with rice wine and vinegar, scraping any browned bits off the bottom. Dissolve the rice flour in a large cup with the chicken broth. Add to the pan with the peanut butter and fish sauce.

Simmer the chicken in sauce: Return the chicken breasts to the pan. Simmer the chicken uncovered for 20 to 25 minutes until the sauce thickens and the chicken is fully cooked. Transfer the chicken to a serving dish and pour the sauce on top. Sprinkle the fresh coriander leaves (cilantro) and ground peanuts as a garnish.

Variation: Pipián Casoy. If you're not crazy about peanuts, try making this dish instead with ground roasted cashews, a beautiful thickener for the sauce. To make cashew paste, place ¼ cup (25 g) roasted cashews in a food processor with 1 tablespoon olive oil. Process until it becomes a smooth paste. Follow the recipe above, substituting cashew butter for peanut butter and ground cashews for ground peanuts.

FRIED CHICKEN PRITONG MANOK

All-American fried chicken is easily "Filipinoed" by the infusion of a piquant *adobo* marinade that flavors the meat instead of relying on a heavily seasoned batter. The reliable three-step breading of flour, egg wash, and Japanese panko bread crumbs really seals in the adobo flavors and gives the chicken a light exterior crunch. My preference for using chicken breast in this dish is not the Filipino standard. Legs, thighs, and wings are always more flavorful and desired by Filipinos over the bland breast meat. However, I love the versatility of breast meat that fits nicely into a modern, hectic schedule. Slice this chicken over a Ceasar salad, cut it into fingers for your kids, or sandwich it in between a crusty roll for a quick, mouthwatering lunch.

Serves 4

2 lbs (900 g) boneless chicken
　breast, skin removed

Marinade

¼ cup (50 ml) soy sauce

3 cloves garlic, minced

½ teaspoon peeled and minced fresh
　ginger

1 conventional lime or calamansi,
　zest and juice

1 tablespoon vinegar

¼ teaspoon freshly ground black
　pepper

Breading

3 cups (750 ml) oil, for frying

1 cup (125 g) all-purpose flour

2 cups (225 g) panko bread crumbs

2 large eggs, beaten

Marinate the chicken: Make the marinade by combining the soy sauce, garlic, ginger, lime zest and juice, vinegar, and pepper in a shallow glass or ceramic dish. Lay the chicken breasts in the dish and marinate for 1 hour, turning the breasts over after 30 minutes.

Bread and fry the chicken: Heat the oil to 350°F (175°C) in a large pot or deep sauté pan. Prepare the breading by gathering separate bowls of flour, bread crumbs, and beaten egg. Dip a chicken breast in the flour and shake to remove any excess. Dip the chicken in the egg, then into the bread crumbs so that it is fully coated. Place in the hot oil and continue breading and cooking the remaining chicken breasts. Do not overcrowd your pan.

Cook the chicken 5 to 7 minutes per side until the coating is golden brown and the chicken is cooked through. A meat thermometer inserted into the breast should read 160°F (72°C). Place the chicken on a serving plate lined with paper towels. Serve while hot.

CHICKEN STEW WITH ROASTED PEPPERS AND POTATOES
APRITADA NGA MANOK

It doesn't get more simple or flavorful than chicken simply seasoned with sweet bell pepper and tomatoes. The addition of potato to this stew makes it a hearty, one-pot meal that really shines when made a day ahead. *Apritada*, like many regional recipes in the Philippines, enjoys the gamut of variations that may include the addition of green peas, olives, liver sauce, or pimentos. My take on *apritada* requires roasting the pepper and charring the tomatoes to intensify their flavors.

Serves 4

2 lbs (900 g) chicken legs or thighs
2 cloves garlic, minced
2 tablespoons soy sauce
1 tablespoon calamansi juice
1 large red bell pepper
2 tomatoes
1 tablespoon olive oil
1 onion, sliced
1 cup (250 ml) Chicken Stock (see page 15)
1 potato, peeled and diced
¼ cup (50 g) green olives
Dash of freshly ground black pepper

Marinate the chicken: Combine the chicken, garlic, soy sauce, and calamansi juice in a large bowl. Toss to combine, cover, and refrigerate for 1 hour.

Roast the pepper and tomatoes:
While the chicken is marinating, roast the bell pepper and tomatoes. Set your oven rack 6 to 8 inches below your broiler. Place your bell pepper and tomatoes on a parchment-lined baking sheet directly under the broiler so that the flame is within a few inches of the vegetables. Blacken the skin on all sides of the pepper and tomatoes. Remove the charred tomatoes and set aside to cool. Peel off the charred skin and coarsely chop.

Place the charred pepper in a bowl and cover the bowl with plastic wrap for 15 minutes to steam, which allows the blackened skin to separate from the flesh. Uncover the pepper and gently rub the skin from the flesh. It should come off easily. Discard the blackened skin, the seeds, and the core. Slice the pepper into large pieces and set aside with the tomatoes.

Cook the chicken: Heat the olive oil in a large sauté pan (3 to 4 quarts/liters) over medium heat. Sauté the onion for 1 to 2 minutes until translucent. Add the chicken with the marinade, roasted pepper, roasted tomatoes, and chicken stock. Simmer for 20 minutes. Add the potato, olives, and pepper. Stir and simmer for 25 minutes until the potato is tender. Ladle onto a serving platter.

BRAISED TURKEY WITH STUFFING PAKSIW NGA PABO

Although Thanksgiving has always been a special gathering in my family, the Friday after was equally filled with fond food memories. My sister and I looked forward to the day that my mom turned Thursday's leftover turkey roast into *paksiw*, a simple, tender, flavor-packed stew. Paksiw means to stew in vinegar, which has something of a harsh inference to it. However, so artful was my mother with her paksiw that I remember it as being smooth and vibrant, never sour. Her trick was to add the leftover bread stuffing to the turkey, which thickened the sauce and mellowed the vinegar. If you happen to have leftover turkey roast, that's what tastes best. But because there aren't too many occasions to have turkey and stuffing lying around the house, this recipe uses smoked turkey legs and can be made the other eleven months of the year.

Serves 6

2½ lbs (1 kg) smoked turkey legs or leftover roasted turkey legs
3 cloves garlic, chopped
4 whole green onions (scallions)
½ teaspoon dried oregano
¼ teaspoon dried thyme
1½ cups (50 g) croutons or pre-pared bread stuffing

1 bay leaf
¾ cup (175 ml) coconut or palm vinegar
2 tablespoons sugar
¼ cup (50 ml) soy sauce
¼ cup (50 ml) oyster sauce
½ teaspoon freshly ground black pepper
6 cups (1½ liters) Chicken Stock (see page 15)

Combine the smoked turkey, garlic, green onions (scallions), dried oregano and thyme, croutons, bay leaf, vinegar, sugar, soy sauce, oyster sauce, pepper, and chicken stock.

Bring the broth to a boil and immediately reduce to a simmer for 45 to 50 minutes until the turkey has become very tender and the sauce has reduced and thickened. Remove and discard the bay leaf. Serve with rice.

DUCK ADOBO WITH PINEAPPLE AND DATES
ADOBONG PATO A LA MONJA

As every Filipino knows, words do not do justice in describing the alchemy of *adobo*. The magic of the Philippines' national dish can only be captured in the permeating smell and unforgettable taste of food transformed by the slow simmering of garlic, soy, vinegar, bay leaf, and peppercorns. As the national dish, adobo is most often made with chicken and/or pork. But as a cooking technique, the five adobo ingredients can be applied to most any food, including vegetables. The classic preparation of Adobo Manok, or chicken adobo, is one of my favorite foods and a regularly scheduled dish on my weekday dinner repertoire. The simple unadorned stew is a quick and zesty standard, subject to regional variations, including the addition of coconut milk, ginger, or citrus juice. Adobo, prepared here "in the style of nuns" or *a la monja*, is an old dish lightly embellished with pineapple and tomato. I have taken the liberty of substituting flavorful Muscovy duck for chicken, a minor departure from the original that only adds to the dish's complexity. In general, I don't like to adobo breast meat because the long stewing time needed to tenderize the leg and thigh inevitably leads to chewy overcooked breasts. Instead, I adobo the legs, thighs, and wings and reserve the breast for a stovetop sear that allows me to crisp the skin, melt the excess fat, and cook the duck breast to a perfect medium doneness.

Makes 4 servings

4 to 5 lbs (approximately 2 kg) Muscovy duck
¼ cup (50 ml) coconut or palm vinegar
3 tablespoons soy sauce
2 bay leaves
4 cloves garlic, peeled
½ teaspoon peeled and minced fresh ginger
¼ teaspoon black peppercorns
2 teaspoons tomato paste
2 tablespoons oyster sauce
2 to 2½ cups (500 to 625 ml) Chicken Stock (see page 15), enough to cover the duck pieces
¼ cup (50 g) diced pineapple
¼ cup (40 g) chopped Chinese red dates (substitute Medjool dates)

Prepare the duck: Remove the innards from the duck cavity. Rinse the duck under cold water and pat dry with paper towels. Cut the duck into six pieces, separating each of the two breasts, thighs, legs, and wings from the carcass. Reserve the carcass for duck stock. Set aside the duck breasts.

Make the adobo: Place the legs, wings, and thighs into a large sauté pan (3 to 4 quarts/liters). Add the vinegar, soy sauce, bay leaves, garlic, ginger, peppercorns, tomato paste, oyster sauce, and chicken stock. Bring the adobo to a boil. Reduce the heat and simmer for 45 minutes covered. Remove the cover and add the pineapple and dates. Simmer uncovered for 20 minutes until the sauce has reduced and thickened. Remove and discard the bay leaf.

Cook the duck breast: While the sauce is reducing, lightly score the skin on the duck breasts in a diagonal cross-hatch pattern. Heat a 10-inch (25-cm) skillet over a medium-high flame. Place the duck breasts in the skillet skin side down, searing the skin until golden brown, reduce the heat to medium, and cook for 7 to 8 minutes. Turn the breasts to cook the other side, 5 to 6 minutes, until the meat reaches medium doneness. A meat thermometer inserted into the center of the breast should read 150 to 155°F (65 to 70°C). Remove the breasts from the pan and let rest for 3 minutes before slicing into thin pieces.

Serve the duck: Place the stewed duck and sliced duck breast on a serving platter. Spoon the adobo sauce over the duck and serve with steamed white rice.

Variation: Classic Filipino Adobo. This classic dish is either made with pork, chicken, or a combination of both and is one of the simplest and most delicious dishes in Filipino cuisine. For a classic *adobo manok*, or chicken adobo, follow the above recipe substituting 2 pounds (900 g) chicken legs, thighs, wings, or any assortment of the three for the duck. If you'd like to enjoy pork in your adobo, use 1 pound (450 g) chicken and 1 pound (450 g) cubed pork roast (pork butt, country rib meat, or belly). Follow the recipe as directed, excluding the tomato paste, pineapple, and dates.

CITRUS-GINGER CHICKEN   INASAL MANOK

Something as simple as broiled chicken can be transformed into a memorable dish with a vibrant marinade and a flavorful dipping sauce. Although this dish is oven-broiled, using smoked paprika adds that incomparable charcoal-grilled element that smells and tastes of summer.

Serves 4

1½ teaspoons peeled and minced fresh ginger
1 small lime, zest and juice
1 small lemon, zest and juice
¼ cup (50 ml) soy sauce
2 tablespoons fish sauce
2 tablespoons mirin
½ teaspoon smoked paprika
2½ lbs (1¼ kg) chicken legs, thighs, or wings (substitute 2 lbs/900 g) chicken breast

Combine the ginger, lime zest and juice, lemon zest and juice, soy sauce, fish sauce, mirin, and paprika in a small bowl. Whisk together to mix well. Place the chicken in a large dish. Pour the marinade over the chicken.

Cover with plastic wrap and refrigerate for 24 hours, turning the chicken over after 12 hours.

Preheat the broiler and set the oven rack to within 6 to 8 inches from the top of the broiler. Prepare a roasting pan fitted with a roasting rack. Arrange the chicken over the rack. Broil the chicken for 10 to 15 minutes until the skin has browned. Turn the oven to 400°F (200°C). Continue baking the chicken for 15 to 20 minutes until the chicken is completely cooked. Your meat thermometer will read at least 165°F (75°C) at the deepest part of the thigh.

DIPPING SAUCE

1 clove garlic, peeled and minced
1 tablespoon soy sauce
1 teaspoon palm vinegar
¼ teaspoon freshly ground black pepper

Combine all the ingredients in a small bowl. Serve alongside the broiled chicken.

STUFFED QUAIL RELLENONG PUGO

This dish is modeled after the more traditional *rellenong manok* (stuffed chicken), a complicated dish that Filipinos reserve for special occasions, celebrations, and fiestas. It requires deboning a whole chicken while keeping the body intact, stuffing it with an elaborate filling of pork, sausage, ham, eggs, vegetables, and cheese, and slowly roasting it until perfectly done. Using semiboneless quail helps make what would normally be a challenging, although rewarding, dish a weekday specialty. I have adapted a brown rice and pork stuffing that is traditionally flavored and balanced with sweet, salty, and savory ingredients, a combination exemplified in Filipino cuisine.

Makes 6 stuffed quail

Stuffing
1 oz (25 g) roasted almonds
1 oz (25 g) green Spanish olives
1 oz (25 g) raisins
1 tablespoon olive oil
1 green onion (scallion), finely
  chopped
2 cloves garlic, minced
4 oz (125 g) ground pork
2 chicken livers, chopped
1 cup (150 g) cooked brown rice
2 teaspoons soy sauce
¼ teaspoon freshly ground black
  pepper

Quail
6 (4 oz/125 g) semiboneless quail
1 tablespoon olive oil
¼ cup (50 ml) rice wine
1½ cups (375 ml) Chicken Stock (see
  page 15)

Make the stuffing: Combine the almonds, olives, and raisins in a food processor. Pulse several times until the mixture is finely chopped. Set aside.

Heat the olive oil in a large skillet over medium heat. Add the green onion (scallion) and garlic.

Cook and stir for 1 minute. Add the ground pork and livers. Cook for 7 to 9 minutes, occasionally stirring and breaking up the meats, until the pork and livers are thoroughly cooked.

Turn off the heat. Add the rice, the almond-raisin mixture, soy sauce, and pepper. Stir to mix well. Set aside to cool before stuffing the quail.

Prepare the quail: The easiest way to bone a quail is to buy one already deboned. That's the honest truth. Look for semiboneless quail, which are whole quail that have the ribcage and spine removed. Only the wing and leg bones remain. If semiboneless quail is not available, you can certainly buy whole quail and debone it yourself, which is not hard once you get the hang of it. I like to butterfly the quail, then debone it. First lay the quail with its legs toward you breastside down. With sharp kitchen shears, cut through the backbone, splitting the quail open. Slide the tip of your boning knife in between the backbones and flesh, carefully separating the meat from the bone. Cut the bones off at the leg, wing, and neck joints. Once deboned, the quail will be butterflied and have only the drumstick and wing bones left.

Stuff the quail: With a semiboneless quail, you merely have to stuff the quail as you would a turkey, through the opening in the body cavity, then sealing the opening shut with toothpicks. If using butterflied quail, first lightly salt and pepper the skin and flesh sides of the quail. Use your hand to form a ping-pong ball–sized amount of rice stuffing and place it in the center of the quail. Bring both sides of the quail up around the stuffing and seal the quail body shut with toothpicks. You'll use 3 to 4 toothpicks per quail. Place the stuffed quail on a plate.

Cook the quail: Heat the olive oil in a large skillet or Dutch oven over high heat. Place the stuffed quail breastside down in the skillet. Sear the quail for 2 to 3 minutes on all sides until the skin is nicely browned. Add the rice wine and chicken stock to the pan. Cover the pan and simmer the quail over medium heat for 10 to 15 minutes until the quail is cooked through. A meat thermometer inserted into the center of the quail should read 165°F (75°C) and the chicken stock will be reduced into a thick sauce. Remove all the toothpicks from the quail. Place the quail whole on a platter. Pour the reduced sauce over quail and serve.

OVEN ROASTED PORK LECHON KAWALI

SUGAR BRAISED PORK HUMBA

BEEF STEW CALDERETA

CORIANDER-CRUSTED BEEF IN BLACK BEAN SAUCE

PORK MEDALLIONS WITH EGGPLANT SOFRITO TAPA NGA BABOY

RIB EYE STEAK AND ONION RINGS BISTEK

CASHEW-CRUSTED LAMB CHOPS LAMB CASOY

BARBECUE PORK RIBS INASAL NGA GUSOK SA BABOY

OXTAIL IN PEANUT SAUCE KARE-KARE

STUFFED BEEF ROLL IN TOMATO SAUCE MORCON

MEAT

Meat to a Filipino typically means one of three things: pork, beef, or goat. Regional meat choices may also include locally raised animals such as sheep and caribou (water buffalo) or the occasional wildlife, such as deer or wild boar. Luckily, methods of meat preparation are not limited. Since the most affordable meats usually tend to be lower in quality, stewing and simmering are common techniques used to tenderize tough chewy cuts. Ham hocks, pork butt, beef chuck, and oxtail are examples of meats that are slowly stewed for a lazy hour or two until they are fork-tender and falling off the bone. However, the nicer pieces of tenderloin, rib eye or sirloin, need only a light infusion of marinade before grilling, stir-frying, or sautéing—quick-cooking techniques that preserve tenderness and flavor.

For the most part, pork dominates Filipino meat consumption except in the Muslim areas of Mindanao where the locals maintain a pork-free diet. Many Filipinos, especially those living in the rural areas of the Philippines untouched by large grocery stores, enjoy backyard bounties that are not limited to vegetable gardens and chickens but also include pigs. One smell that is certain to take me back to the island of Cebu in an instant is the smoky aroma of *lechon*, a roasted suckling pig, the quintessential Filipino fiesta dish that my father still makes on his homemade outdoor spit for special occasions. Admittedly, roasting a whole pig is not a light task, and likely not something you will be whipping up for a weekday dinner. *Lechon Kawali* is the manageable (although still not quick), stove-cooked version of this spit-roasted delicacy that yields the two most important elements of roasted pig: tender meat and *sitsaron*, crispy skin. *Humba* is, in my opinion, the cat's meow of pork recipes in this collection: mahogany-colored chunks of pork simmered with fermented black beans, brown sugar, and vinegar served over Maja Blanca Mais (coconut corn pudding, page 139) made it the best-selling dish at my restaurant.

Beef made its way to the Philippines with the Spanish who, at great expense and effort, imported cattle from their Mexican territories. *Caldereta* is a classic Filipino stew traditionally made with delicious goat meat but here presented with chunks of flavorful beef and enriched with Chicken Liver Mousse (page 32) for a sauce that gives new meaning to the word *velvety*. Of course, included in this chapter is *Bistek*, a Filipino staple of marinated steak with onions, pairing two simple ingredients that complement each other so well. My version features crispy fried onion rings and a red wine–soy sauce, two nontraditional elements in Filipino *bistek* that nonetheless retain an undeniably Filipino flavor print. Spicy food is not a Filipino standard except on Palawan and Mindanao, the southern islands closest to Malaysia and Indonesia, and the Bicol region of Luzon where the locals often use native chiles (*sili*) to flavor their food. I have included one nontraditional, chile-spiced dish in Coriander-Crusted Beef in Black Bean Sauce, a grilled steak tossed with what I think may become your newest favorite barbecue sauce: an amazing melt of fermented black beans, hoisin sauce, and sambal ulek that quietly explodes with flavor and heat. This sauce holds a wealth of delicious possibilities when served with chicken, pork tenderloin, or scallops.

I was extremely hard-pressed to find authentic Filipino lamb recipes since it just isn't a part of mainstream Filipino cuisine. The nontraditional Lamb Casoy (or Cashew-Crusted Lamb Racks) is my way of enjoying the distinctive flavor of lamb with a Filipino twist.

OVEN ROASTED PORK LECHON KAWALI

From the most modest gathering to the elaborately prepared holiday fiesta, *lechon*, or whole spit-roasted suckling pig, symbolizes the pinnacle of Filipino hospitality and generosity when it comes to sharing life's rewards with family and friends. The time and care taken in preparing and roasting a lechon to perfection is rewarded with dark brown, crispy skin (most Filipinos would agree that the skin is the best part) covering juicy flavorful meat that is nearly falling off the bone onto your plate. Spit roasting your own pig is a weighty endeavor requiring heavy equipment, more than a few helping hands, and a majority of the day devoted to the task. Luckily, there is a more manageable alternative with Lechon Kawali, an oven roasted version of lechon. *Kawali*, meaning "pan" in Tagalog, is where the pork is first simmered until tender before being quickly fried to crisp the skin. I prefer the one-step ease of oven-roasting that yields the same results with much less mess and fuss. Traditionally, a liver sauce is served with both spit-roasted lechon and the kawali version, although I like to put a few other dipping sauces on the table for variety.

Serves 4

2 lbs (900 g) pork belly or pork
  shoulder, skin on
2 tablespoons kosher or
  sea salt
2 small bay leaves
4 cloves garlic, chopped
1 small onion, diced
¼ cup (50 ml) soy sauce

Lechon Dipping Sauce I: Liver Sauce
¼ cup (50 g) Chicken Liver Mousse
  (see page 32) or liver pâté
¼ cup (50 ml) water
1 green onion (scallion),
  chopped
1 clove garlic, minced
1 tablespoon calamansi juice
½ teaspoon soy sauce
Dash of freshly ground black pepper

Lechon Dipping Sauce II:
Garlic and Soy
2 tablespoons soy sauce
2 teaspoons lime juice
1 clove garlic, minced
¼ teaspoon sambal ulek or chopped
  Thai chile

Marinate the pork: Thoroughly dry the skin of the pork with paper towels and score the skin every ½ inch (13 cm) with a sharp knife.

Generously rub the salt into the skin; this will draw out as much moisture as possible. Combine the bay leaves, garlic, onion, and soy sauce in a shallow baking dish. Gently place the pork in the dish meat side down so that the skin remains dry. Marinate uncovered in the refrigerator for 1 hour.

Roast the pork: Preheat the oven to 425°F (220°C). Line a roasting pan with aluminum foil and fit with a roasting rack. Remove the pork from the marinade and place on the rack. Discard the marinade. Again, pat the skin dry with paper towels; don't worry if you rub off some of the salt. It is very important that the skin is dry while cooking so that it crisps and puffs. Roast the pork for 1½ to 2 hours until the internal temperature of the pork reaches 155°F (70°C). Let the pork rest for 15 minutes before slicing.

To make dipping sauce I or II: Place all the ingredients in a small saucepan. Cook over medium heat, stirring occasionally, for 10 to 15 minutes, until the sauce thickens. Pour the sauce into a bowl and serve with the lechon.

SUGAR BRAISED PORK HUMBA

The immense power of food to comfort and caress the human soul, even by the mere smell, is epitomized by this dish. Traditionally made with ham hocks, *humba* (shown opposite) is braised in a sweet-tangy liquid of fermented black beans, vinegar, and brown sugar that transforms the meat into tender mahogany. Although ham hocks undeniably produce a more robust humba, they are not the most practical cut, having very little meat under thick layers of skin and fat. Pork butt, also called pork shoulder, is a leaner, healthier substitute that gives you 100 percent of the flavor without the added guilt.

Serves 6

2½ lbs (1¼ kg) pork shoulder, cut into 1-in (2½-cm) cubes
¼ cup (25 g) dried fermented black beans
4 dried shiitake mushrooms
¾ cup (150 g) dark brown sugar
½ cup (125 ml) palm or coconut vinegar
¼ cup (50 ml) soy sauce
2 bay leaves

2 cloves garlic, peeled
1 teaspoon peeled and minced fresh ginger
¼ teaspoon freshly ground black pepper
3 tablespoons oyster sauce
3 to 4 cups (750 ml to 1 liter) Chicken or Beef Stock (see pages 15 and 14)

Place all the ingredients in a large pot. There should be enough stock to cover the pork by 1 inch (2½ cm). Bring the mixture to a boil. Skim off and discard any foam that rises to the surface.

Cover the pot and reduce the heat to a low simmer for 2 to 2½ hours until the pork is tender. Remove the cover and increase the heat to medium-high. Cook for another 30 minutes until the liquid is reduced to a thick sauce. Remove and discard the bay leaves. Serve with Maja Blanca Mais (page 139).

BEEF STEW CALDERETA

With beef stews coming in all shapes and sizes, the Filipino version, called *caldereta*, has its own unique standards that set it apart from the rest. The traditional meat of choice isn't actually beef, but goat, which for more than half the world's population, is everyday food. Like beef, lamb, or venison, goat meat has a distinct flavor and is tender and sumptuous when properly cooked. Because of goat's limited availability in the United States, I more often make this recipe with either beef or lamb with stellar results. Caldereta also features the Filipino method of adding just a touch of liver to thicken the braising sauce. The liver is usually in the form of chopped beef or goat liver, or a prepared liverwurst. I use the Chicken Liver Mousse (page 32) as a silky, concentrated thickener that adds luscious flavor and incomparable richness without masking the stew's natural brightness.

Serves 4

1 lb (450 g) beef chuck, cut into 1-in (2½-cm) cubes (substitute young goat meat, less than 1 year old, from the shoulder, shank, or leg)
2 tablespoons calamansi juice
¼ cup (50 ml) rice wine
3 tablespoons soy sauce
2 cloves garlic, minced
1 tablespoon olive oil
1 small onion, sliced
3 tablespoons tomato paste

¼ cup (50 g) Chicken Liver Mousse (see page 32)
4 cups (1 liter) Beef Stock (see page 14)
1 bay leaf
½ cup (75 g) green olives
½ cup (65 g) grated Edam cheese

Combine the beef, calamansi juice, rice wine, soy sauce, and garlic in a large bowl and toss to mix. Cover with plastic wrap and refrigerate for 1 hour.

Heat the olive oil in a large pot (3 to 4 quarts/liters) over medium heat. Add the onion. Cook and stir for 3 to 4 minutes until onion begins to brown. Add the beef with the marinade, tomato paste, chicken liver mousse, beef stock, and bay leaf. Bring the mixture to a boil. Using a ladle, skim off and discard any foam that rises to the surface. Reduce the heat to a simmer and cover. Simmer for 1½ to 2 hours until the beef is very tender when pierced with a fork. Stir in the green olives and remove from the heat. Remove and discard the bay leaf. Sprinkle the stew with the grated cheese and serve hot.

CORIANDER-CRUSTED BEEF IN BLACK BEAN SAUCE

I first realized the culinary importance of fermented black beans in college when I tried cooking *humba* (page 108) for the first time, substituting a can of Mexican black beans for the real thing. Naturally, I was sorely disappointed by the results, which bore no resemblance to the humba of my heart. Without that distinct saltiness and rich flavor, my humba was shallow and incomplete. These small fermented soybeans are an essential flavor component in Asian cooking that cannot be replaced. I prefer using the semidried beans packaged in vacuum-sealed plastic instead of the canned variety, which definitely retains some of the metallic aftertaste of the tin. This black bean sauce is a treasure to have in your refrigerator. It serves as an amazing barbecue sauce basted over chicken or beef, and as a quick stir-fry sauce for meats, vegetables, or noodles.

Serves 4

Black Bean Sauce: makes 2½ cups (625 ml)

1 cup (125 g) fermented black soy beans
2 cloves garlic, peeled
1 cup (250 ml) hoisin sauce
2 teaspoons dried red pepper flakes
1 cup (250 ml) light corn syrup
1 teaspoon peeled and grated fresh ginger
2 teaspoons balsamic vinegar
1 tablespoon soy sauce

Coriander-Crusted Beef

2 tablespoons crushed coriander seeds
1 lb (450 g) beef rib eye or sirloin
1 teaspoon vegetable oil
1 bunch (approximately ¼ lb/125 g) watercress, rinsed and woody stems removed

Make the sauce: Combine the fermented black beans and garlic in a food processor and pulse 10 to 15 times until finely chopped. Scrape into a saucepan and add the remaining ingredients. Simmer for 15 to 20 minutes until thick. Remove from the heat and cool completely. Store in an airtight container in the refrigerator for up to 2 weeks.

Prepare the coriander-crusted beef: Place the crushed coriander seeds in a large, plastic freezer bag. Place the beef in the plastic bag and press the crushed coriander seeds evenly onto the meat. Remove the beef from the bag.

Heat the oil in a large skillet over high heat. When you see the oil smoking, carefully place the beef in the pan. Sear both sides of the beef for 3 to 4 minutes until the beef is well browned and the steak is cooked to rare (145°F/63°C). Remove the steak from the pan and allow the meat to rest for 5 minutes. Slice the steak thinly across the grain. Heat the same pan on medium-high heat. Return the steak to the pan and stir-fry for 1 minute. Add 2 cups of the black bean sauce and cook for another 2 to 3 minutes. Remove the pan from the heat and add the watercress to the pan. Toss to combine the greens with the beef and sauce. Serve immediately.

PORK MEDALLIONS WITH EGGPLANT SOFRITO TAPA NGA BABOY

There are two schools of thought when it comes to Filipino *tapa*: dry and wet. Both techniques call for thinly sliced meat that has been heavily marinated with a base of soy, sugar, and salt. To further preserve the meat, the slices are laid out for several hours in the sun to dry into jerkylike strips that can be stored or eaten after a quick panfry. The wet tapa method, as demonstrated here, skips the drying step so that the meat is tender when cooked. Tapa is a breakfast essential in the Philippines paired with *sinangag*, Garlic Fried Rice (page 79) and *itlog*, sunny-side up eggs, a triumvirate colloquially shortened to *tapsilog*. Although it requires a little preparation, tapa makes a deliciously different alternative to bacon or sausage for breakfast. I especially like pairing it with chopped green olives or this eggplant sofrito for a substantial dish worthy of attention at lunch or dinner.

Serves 4

Marinade

5 tablespoons soy sauce
1 tablespoon vinegar
2 teaspoons sweet soy
¼ teaspoon sambal ulek or dried red
   pepper flakes
1½ lbs (675 g) pork loin

Eggplant Sofrito

3 tablespoons olive oil
1 small yellow onion, chopped
1 clove garlic, minced
1 tomato, chopped
¼ lb (125 g) eggplant, cut into ½-in
   (1⅓-cm) cubes
¼ cup (50 ml) Chicken Stock (see
   page 15)
2 tablespoons soy sauce
½ teaspoon freshly ground black
   pepper

Marinate the pork: Combine the soy sauce, vinegar, sweet soy, and sambal ulek in a large bowl. Whisk to dissolve. Slice the pork into very thin medallions and place in a baking dish. Pour the marinade over the pork, making sure that each slice is covered with marinade. Cover the dish with plastic wrap and refrigerate overnight.

Cook the tapa: Heat a skillet over a high flame. Lightly oil the pan with cooking spray or olive oil. When the pan begins smoking add the tapa slices. Do not overcrowd the pan. Cook the tapa for 3 to 4 minutes per side until medallions are fully cooked and the sugar from the brine caramelizes. Dry the tapa on paper towels. Lay the tapa on a serving platter.

Prepare the eggplant sofrito: Heat the olive oil over medium heat in a large (3 to 4 quarts/liters) sauté pan. Sauté the onion, garlic, and tomato together for 3 to 4 minutes until the tomato collapses. Add the eggplant and chicken stock. Cook for 7 to 8 minutes until eggplant is tender. Season with soy sauce and pepper. Serve alongside the cooked tapa.

RIB EYE STEAK AND ONION RINGS BISTEK

There is something about the simplicity of a perfectly grilled steak—lightly dusted with freshly ground peppercorns and cooked to perfect juiciness—that borders on art. Although a good cut of steak needs nothing more than salt and pepper to accentuate its natural flavors, Filipino *bistek* takes the meat one step further with a light marinade, originally intended as both a flavor agent and a tenderizer. Bistek traditionally uses a tougher cut of meat such as flank, skirt, or strip steak, which requires at least an hour of marinating time. Spending just a little more money on a nicer cut like rib eye or sirloin will ensure that your bistek is tender and juicy. This recipe strays from tradition with the addition of red wine, a very un-Filipino ingredient to add to a marinade. But it works nicely as a complex acid that eventually develops the steak sauce. Bistek is usually stir-fried but I find the incomparable flavor of a charcoal grill an asset to the dish. A stovetop grill pan is certainly a rainy day or winter alternative.

Serves 4

Marinade
1 clove garlic, minced
3 tablespoons soy sauce
1 small lime, zest and juice
1 tablespoon brown sugar
¼ cup (50 ml) red wine
¼ cup (50 ml) Beef Stock (see page 14)
2 lbs (900 g) rib eye, cut into ½-in (1⅓-cm)-thick steaks
1 teaspoon olive oil
1 small onion, finely diced
Salt and freshly ground black pepper, to taste

Marinate the steak: Combine the garlic, soy sauce, lime zest and juice, brown sugar, red wine, and beef stock together in a large baking dish. Add the steaks to the mixture and marinate for 10 minutes on each side.

Grill the steak: Heat the grill over medium-high heat. Lightly brush oil on the grates to ensure your steaks do not stick. Remove the steaks from the marinade, reserving the liquid, and grill the steaks for 4 to 6 minutes per side for medium rare to medium doneness (145 to 155°F/63 to 70°C). Remove the steaks from the grill onto a plate and let rest for 5 minutes before slicing. Slice steak into thin strips and arrange on a serving platter. Keep warm.

Make the pan sauce: Heat the olive oil in a small sauté pan over medium-high heat. Add the diced onion and sauté for 2 minutes until translucent. Pour the reserved marinade into the sauté pan and cook over high heat for 5 to 7 minutes until the sauce reduces and thickens. Season with salt and pepper and pour over the grilled steaks. Serve immediately with the crispy fried onion rings.

ONION RINGS

3 cups (750 ml) oil, for frying
1 cup (225 g) all-purpose flour
½ cup (50 g) cornstarch
2 teaspoons baking powder
2 cups (500 ml) cold water
2 large onions, sliced into ¼-in (6½-mm) rings

Preheat the oil in a deep pot (3 to 4 quarts/liters) to 350°F/175°C.

To make the batter, combine the flour, cornstarch, baking powder, and cold water in a large bowl. Use a wooden spoon or spatula to lightly stir until just combined. Do not overbeat the batter. Dip the onion rings into the batter and allow the excess batter to drip back into the bowl. Place the onion rings in the hot oil, making sure that the pot is not overcrowded. Fry the onion rings until golden brown on all sides. Drain on paper towels and serve immediately with steak.

CASHEW-CRUSTED LAMB CHOPS LAMB CASOY

In 1609, Antonio de Morga, a Spanish administrator in the Philippines, noted in his famous book *Sucesos de las Islas Filipinas*, not only the islands' lack of sheep but the failure of imported sheep to thrive. Still today, lamb is not common fare on most Filipino tables. But with it being readily available and affordable here in the States, I couldn't resist pairing lamb's tender meat and distinctive flavor with Filipino ingredients. *Casoy*, or cashews, made a long journey from their native Brazil to the Philippines via Portuguese traders, who first introduced the delicious nut to the Asian continent through India. Along with peanuts and pili nuts, cashews are frequently used in Filipino dishes. Although typically reserved for desserts and sweets, nuts succeed in crossing over into savory territory, as they do here, crushed with mustard, olives, garlic, and ginger. Pair this dish with *Guinataan* (page 139), *Pritong Saging* (page 36), or Palm Hearts and Apple Salad (page 71) for a complementary range of flavors and textures.

Serves 4

1 cup (150 g) roasted cashews
¼ cup (50 g) green olives
1 clove garlic, peeled
2 tablespoons mustard
1 teaspoon peeled and chopped
   fresh ginger
1 Australian or New Zealand lamb
   rack with 8 cutlets (2½ to 3 lbs/
   1¼ to 1½ kg), frenched
Salt and freshly ground black pepper
   to taste

Make the cashew crust: Place the cashews, olives, garlic, mustard, and ginger in a food processor fitted with a metal blade. Pulse the mixture 10 to 15 times until the cashews are finely chopped but not a paste. Transfer the mixture to a bowl and set aside.

Prepare the lamb: Preheat the oven to 375°F (190°C). Cut away the excess fat "cap" that covers the meaty chops, leaving just a thin layer of fat to keep the meat moist during roasting. Season the lamb with salt and pepper on all sides. Press the cashew crust onto the fat side of the lamb.

Cook the lamb: Place the lamb crust side up in a roasting pan fitted with a roasting rack. Roast the lamb for 30 to 35 minutes until the meat thermometer reading in the center of the "eye" of the meat reads 145°F (63°C) for medium rare. Remove the lamb from the oven and loosely cover it with aluminum foil, allowing the meat to rest for 5 to 7 minutes before slicing between the bones to separate the chops.

Frenched Rack of Lamb

A frenched lamb rack means that the fat and sinew have been trimmed from around the rib bones so that they are attractively clean and exposed. Save yourself the trouble and ask your butcher to take care of this step for you. If attempting to clean your lamb at home, the procedure is relatively simple. You'll need a boning knife or a thin-blade utility knife to easily maneuver around the bones. Start by holding the lamb upright, the ribs pointing up. Place your knife at the top of a rib and cut down along the side of each rib bone until you reach the fat cap that covers the meaty chop. Once you've cut away the fat and sinew between the bones, use your knife to scrape the bones clean.

BARBECUE PORK RIBS   INASAL NGA GUSOK SA BABOY

While preparing for this book, I recently read one of my old journals from 1986, during my first visit to the Philippines. In describing the short walk from the airplane to the terminal as we disembarked, I scribbled my first impressions of the islands as "hot & humid . . . smells like barbecue." And sure enough, the nose knows. *Inasal* or *inihaw* is Filipino barbecue, the common method of grilling or broiling food over an open flame that is so central to Filipino cookery that the smell permeates the island air. Very popular with street-food vendors and *carindarias* (roadside food stalls), Filipino barbecue isn't just limited to grilled meats or chicken but includes whimsical dishes such as *banana-cue*, ripe plantains coated in sugar, *kamote-cue*, grilled sweet potato, and *adidas*, grilled chicken feet.

Serves 4
3 cloves garlic, minced
1 green onion (scallion), chopped
¼ cup (50 ml) balsamic vinegar
¼ cup (50 ml) honey
¼ cup (50 ml) soy sauce
2 tablespoons mustard
1 teaspoon dried red pepper flakes
½ teaspoon five-spice powder
2½ lbs (1¼ kg) pork ribs

Combine the garlic, green onion (scallion), vinegar, honey, soy sauce, mustard, dried red pepper flakes, and five-spice powder together in a bowl and whisk to dissolve the flavors together. Place the ribs in a large pan and pour the marinade over the ribs. Cover with plastic wrap and refrigerate. Marinate the ribs for 24 hours, turning the ribs after 12 hours so that both sides of the slab are marinated.

Preheat your grill over medium-high heat. Oil the grates. Remove the ribs from the marinade and place the slab on the hottest part of the grill. Discard the marinade. Sear the ribs over high heat for 3 to 5 minutes per side so that the sugar from the marinade begins to caramelize and brown. Move the ribs to a lower heat section of the grill. Cook the ribs over low-medium heat for 1 to 1½ hours until the meat is tender and easily pulls away from the bone.

OXTAIL IN PEANUT SAUCE   KARE-KARE

Oxtail is a cut of beef often misrepresented as inferior in cut and quality, which is not at all the case. I love serving oxtail because my guests are always pleasantly surprised by the tenderness and flavor that so differs from other more expensive beef cuts. *Kare-Kare* is an oxtail stew flavored with a complex peanut sauce that is both spicy and savory. What I love about Filipino cuisine is its ability to take simple everyday dishes and make them multidimensional with balanced layers of flavors. Serve this stew with fried onion rings (page 112) for a textural interplay of tender and crispy.

Serves 4

Peanut Sauce: makes ½ cup (125 ml)
2 tablespoons creamy peanut butter
1 tablespoon miso
1 tablespoon chopped green onion
  (scallion)
1 tablespoon fish sauce
1 clove garlic, peeled
1 teaspoon peeled and chopped
  fresh ginger
1 teaspoon sambal ulek
1 teaspoon shrimp paste
¼ cup (50 ml) coconut milk

Oxtail Stew
1 tablespoon olive oil
2 lbs (900 g) oxtail, cut into 2-in
  (5-cm) pieces
¼ cup (50 ml) rice wine
5 to 6 cups (1¼ to 1½ liters)
  water
¼ lb (125 g) green beans
¼ lb eggplant (125 g),
  cut into 1-in
  (2½-cm) cubes

Make the sauce: Combine all the ingredients in a food processor or blender. Blend until smooth. Set aside. You can make this peanut sauce ahead of time and keep it in the refrigerator for up to 1 week.

Make the stew: Heat the oil in a large pot over high heat. When the oil begins to smoke carefully add the oxtail. Sear each side 3 to 4 minutes until all sides are well browned. Add the rice wine to deglaze the pan. Add the water so that the oxtail is completely covered. Bring to a boil and skim off any foam that rises to the surface.

Cover and reduce the heat to a simmer. Cook the oxtail for 3 to 3½ hours until the oxtail meat is very tender and easily pulls away from the bone. Add the peanut sauce, green beans, and eggplant. Simmer for another 10 to 12 minutes until the vegetables are tender. Serve with crispy fried onion rings (page 112).

STUFFED BEEF ROLL IN TOMATO SAUCE MORCON

This fiesta dish of rolled steak stuffed with a hodgepodge of sweet and savory ingredients was not a common sight on our buffet table when I was growing up, which was disappointing once I had the pleasure of tasting *morcon*. Slices of tender beef beautifully wrapped around a steaming center filling of eggs, sausages, and olives with a little of the tangy tomato sauce spooned over the top made for an exciting departure from the commonly seen *adobo*, *pancit*, and *inasal* that graced our table. It may seem like an involved dish, but it's actually quite simple to put together once you have the ingredients assembled. Beef is the standard for this dish, but I've also made it with a roast cut of pork with delicious results.

Serves 4

1½ lbs (675 g) flank steak

Stuffing

1 teaspoon paprika
1 teaspoon salt
½ teaspoon freshly ground black
   pepper
3 cloves garlic, minced
6 oz (175 g) buffalo mozzarella,
   sliced
2 slices bacon, chopped
2 green onions (scallions), chopped
8 oz (225 g) mushrooms, sliced
½ cup (75 g) chopped green olives
3 oz (85 g) chorizo de Bilbao
3 large hard-boiled eggs, halved

Sauce

1 tablespoon grapeseed oil
¼ cup (50 ml) rice wine
1 can (24 oz/680 g) diced tomatoes
1 teaspoon dried red pepper flakes
1 tablespoon soy sauce
1 tablespoon fish sauce
1 bay leaf
1 cup (250 ml) Beef or Chicken Stock
   (see pages 14 and 15)

Prepare the steak: Butterfly your flank steak by slicing through the center of the steak horizontally, so that you have two large thin halves that open like a book. Be sure to leave one long edge of the steak uncut to hold the halves together. Place a large piece of plastic wrap on top of the butterflied steak and use a meat mallet to pound the meat to even thickness. Remove and discard the plastic wrap. You should have one large thin piece of steak, roughly 10 inches (25 cm) across and 9 inches (23 cm) wide.

Fill the steak: Evenly sprinkle the topside of the steak with the paprika, salt, pepper, and garlic. Lay the slices of mozzarella horizontally across the center of the steak. Sprinkle the chopped bacon, spring onions (scallions), mushrooms, and green olives evenly over the cheese. Down the center of the steak lay the links of chorizo and eggs in a row. Pull the bottom edge of the steak tightly over the filling and roll up the meat. Secure the morcon closed with kitchen twine or pandan leaves.

Cook the roll: Heat the grapeseed oil in a large (4 to 5 quarts/liters) sauté pan or Dutch oven over high heat. Once the oil is smoking, add the beef to the pan. Brown the meat well on all sides, 1 to 2 minutes per side. Remove the browned meat to a plate. Add the rice wine to the pan and scrape off any browned bits into the pan. Add the tomatoes, dried red pepper flakes, soy sauce, fish sauce, bay leaf, and beef stock to the pan. Return the meat to the pan and cover. Lower the heat to medium and simmer for 1 to 1½ hours, turning over the beef roll halfway through cooking, until the beef is tender.

Serve the morcon by removing the roll from the sauce onto a cutting board. Cut off and discard the kitchen twine. Slice the beef roll into ½-inch (13-mm)-thick slices and place on a serving platter. Remove the bay leaf from the sauce and discard. Spoon the sauce over the sliced morcon and serve immediately.

SOFT-SHELL CRAB IN SPICY COCONUT SAUCE ALIMASAG NGA MAY GATA

MILKFISH WITH PILI NUT STUFFING INASAL NGA BANGUS

WHOLE ROASTED RED SNAPPER

MAHI MAHI IN GINGER-MISO BROTH PESA NGA MAY MISU

SWEET-AND-SOUR SKATE WING ESCABECHE NGA ISDA

CABBAGE-WRAPPED TILAPIA IN COCONUT MILK SINANGLAY

GRILLED GROUPER WITH EGGPLANT-PRUNE COMPOTE INASAL NGA LAPU LAPU

RAINBOW TROUT STUFFED WITH KABOCHA SQUASH AND WATER SPINACH

BATTERED FRIED SHRIMP HIPON REBOSADO

CRAB AND EGGPLANT TORTE TORTANG ALAMANG

GREEN LIP MUSSELS WITH MISO GUISADONG TAHONG NGA MAY MISU

SEAFOOD

With over seven thousand islands in its chain, the Philippines is the second largest archipelago in the world, which naturally explains why the surrounding seas are hardly an idle landscape but a vital resource teeming with life. When it comes to edible delights, the waters are abundant with fish, shellfish, and seaweed, providing the majority of Filipinos with their primary source of protein. The only problem that this poses, for those of us living thousands of miles away in landlocked areas, is matching the freshness and variety of sea life so easily attainable to those on the islands. This chapter's anthology covers the gamut of seafood available, regardless of your proximity to a coastline.

One of the challenges of a Filipino-American kitchen far from the homeland is balancing authenticity with availability. In reconciling this dilemma, I've always preferred freshness over tradition, especially where seafood is concerned. Milkfish *bangus*, with its forked tail, distinctive flavor, and abundance of bones, is widely consumed on the islands and considered the national fish of the Philippines. However, even in a large metropolitan city like Chicago, I've had a hard time finding fresh *bangus* outside of the Filipino market, and more often it has been previously frozen then thawed. If you do happen to luck out with an Asian market of substance, you may find fresh milkfish, but more often you will find it frozen, smoked *tinapa*, butterflied, or already cut into steaks. Bangus is featured in this collection, stuffed with a deliciously simple filling of candied pili nuts, shallots, and ginger.

The stuffed rainbow trout was my sous chef's invention, a blockbuster hit of rainbow trout fillets filled with kabocha squash *calabasa* and *adobo* water spinach *kangkong*, elegantly rolled for stunning presentation. *Escabeche*, although Spanish in name, borrows the classic sweet-and-sour combination made famous by the Chinese, but with its own Filipino identity. I've made escabeche with countless varieties of fish and I always come back to skate wing; this sweet fish has an outstanding delicacy that beautifully complements the pineapple and fermented black beans flavoring the sauce.

I certainly know how squeamish some people can be over the idea of preparing whole fish. But if you let your fishmonger do the dirty work of cleaning and scaling your fish for the Whole Roasted Red Snapper, this dish is quite literally a snap. I can't tell you how quickly people get over seeing the head and tail when diving in for a second helping. The Inasal Nga Lapu Lapu (grilled grouper) and Pesa nga may Misu both feature a fermented soy bean paste called misu (you may know it as miso) to flavor the fish for a unique richness that goes far beyond salty.

Alimasag, or blue crab, is abundant in Philippine waters, which is why *Alimasag nga may Gata* is featured using soft-shelled crab cooked in coconut milk—a must-try dish during the summer molting season. Shrimp is another seafood staple. Buying your shrimp with the shell on will allow you to make Shrimp Stock (page 14), a quick and handy flavor booster to keep in your refrigerator or freezer. The peeled shrimp can then be used for Hipon Rebosado, fried shrimp covered in a light batter, or as a substitute for crab in the Gata recipe. Both are quick dishes that are easy to put together during the week. The *Guisadong Tahong nga may Misu* is a typical preparation for mussels. I love using plump and meaty green lip mussels from New Zealand, which are usually frozen on the half-shell. Fresh black mussels are equally delicious and add extra flavor when they release their liquor into the sauce, making an almost drinkable adobo. So have plenty of sticky white rice or bread to sop up every last drop.

SOFT-SHELL CRAB IN SPICY COCONUT SAUCE
ALIMASAG NGA MAY GATA

The Philippines is one Southeast Asian country that has kept its culinary distance from the exuberant use of chiles. Playing more of a regional role on the southern islands of Palawan and Mindanao and the northern Bicol peninsula are *siling habas* or *siling labuyo*, the local green and red hot chile peppers used to add fire to everyday specialties. Here we have soft-shell crab and sweet corn flavored with a paste of fiery, red siling labuyo (also called bird peppers or Thai chiles), garlic, and vinegar. If fresh chiles aren't available, *sambal ulek* chili paste is a terrific and convenient understudy. As with every *gata*, there's an ample supply of coconut milk in this dish to tame the wild heat of the chiles. Pair this with the Coconut-Garlic Mashed Potatoes (page 142) for a brilliant match.

Serves 4

*Garlic Chili Paste: makes about 1
    heaping tablespoon*
1 Thai chile, stem removed
1 small clove garlic, peeled
1 teaspoon peeled and grated fresh
    ginger
1 teaspoon olive oil
1 teaspoon coconut vinegar or palm
    vinegar
Pinch of sugar

Crab
1 cup (125 g) frozen corn
1 cup (130 g) all-purpose flour
4 soft-shell crabs, already cleaned
1 tablespoon olive oil
1 small tomato, diced
½ cup (125 ml) coconut milk
½ cup (125 ml) Fish or Shrimp Stock
    (see page 14)
1 tablespoon fish sauce
1 green onion (scallion), thinly
    sliced
½ teaspoon toasted sesame seeds

Make the chili paste: Place the chile, garlic, ginger, oil, vinegar, and sugar in a mortar and mash into a smooth paste with the pestle. Set aside.

Cook the crab: Place the flour on a plate and dredge the soft-shell crabs on both sides; shake off the excess flour. Heat the remaining olive oil in a large skillet over medium-high heat. When the oil is hot, gently place the crabs in the pan. Panfry the crab for 3 to 4 minutes per side until golden brown. Remove the crabs from the pan and place on a serving dish.

Add the tomato and corn kernels to the pan and sauté for 2 minutes. Add the coconut milk, fish or shrimp stock, garlic chili paste, and fish sauce. Simmer for 3 to 5 minutes until the coconut milk begins to reduce to a thick sauce. Pour the coconut sauce over the crabs and sprinkle with the sliced green onion (scallion) and toasted sesame seeds.

How to Clean Soft-Shell Crab
One of summer's culinary highlights is soft-shell crab season. Blue crabs molt from May to September and in shedding their hard shells become tender and almost entirely edible, shell and all. The ingredients list calls for pre-cleaned soft-shell crabs since you'll more often find soft-shell crabs in many of the large grocery stores conveniently prepared for cooking. But to ensure freshness, live crabs are best to use, although they are sometimes difficult to find.

If you are comfortable cooking live lobster or blue crab, cleaning and cooking soft-shell crab shouldn't be too far from your comfort zone. Only minimal preparation is required. First, take a pair of sharp kitchen shears and cut off the head of the crab, right behind the eyes and mouth. Then gently lift one point of the crab's top shell. Underneath you'll find spongy, grayish-white gills; pull these off and discard. Lift the other point of the crab's shell and repeat the process. Finally, turn the crab over and pull or cut off the belly flap, called the apron. In a female crab, the apron will be heart-shaped; in a male crab it is thin and pointed. Now the crab is ready to cook.

MILKFISH WITH PILI NUT STUFFING INASAL NGA BANGUS

Bangus, or milkfish, is a popular commercially farmed fish in the Philippines that is usually found in ample supply at the Asian market. Although it involves more work, I love stuffing whole bangus; it requires the fish to be "dressed," that is, completely cleaned (scaled, gutted, and gilled) with the head and tail left intact. There's also the exercise of butterflying the fish and removing the spine and pinbones before stuffing, which makes eating the unencumbered fish all the more enjoyable. If the head and tail are too much for you, fillets are the convenient way to go. With a buttery nut mixture of pili nuts and shallots sandwiched in between the fillets, this is a dish that will not disappoint. Plain pili nuts are hard to find, even in a major city like Chicago that has a substantial Asian population. More often, I find pili nuts in a candied brittle with a crunchy caramel coating that gives this dish just the right amount of sweetness. Don't fret over pili nuts if you can't find them; macadamia nuts are comparable in terms of taste and texture. Substitute Adobo-Flavored Pecans (page 33) for a sensational taste.

Serves 4

2 lbs (900 g) whole milkfish, dressed, deboned, and butterflied

Pili Nut Stuffing
2 shallots, thinly sliced
1 teaspoon peeled and minced fresh ginger
1 clove garlic, chopped
¼ cup (25 g) candied pili nuts
1 teaspoon fish sauce
Dash of salt and freshly ground black pepper
3 *calamansi*, halved
½ cup (15 g) fresh coriander leaves (cilantro)

Make the stuffing: Combine the shallots, ginger, garlic, pili nuts, and fish sauce in a bowl and toss together.

Stuff the fish: Lay the butterflied milkfish open on your work surface. Sprinkle with the salt, pepper, and squeeze the calamansi juice on the fillets. Lay the fresh coriander leaves (cilantro) leaves along the back. Spoon the shallot-nut mixture generously onto the bottom fillet. Fold the top fillet over the filling and secure it closed with toothpicks or by tying the fish closed with kitchen twine.

Cook the fish: When hot, lightly oil the grates to prevent sticking. Gently place the fish on the grill and cook for 8 to 10 minutes per side over a medium flame until the fish is completely cooked and the filling is heated through. Place the fish on a platter; remove and discard the toothpicks or twine. Serve immediately.

How to Butterfly a Fish
A butterflied fish is one that is completely cleaned and deboned and has the fillets attached along the back, keeping the whole fish in one neat piece. Rinse the milkfish well under cold water and pat dry with paper towels. Cut off the side, belly, and dorsal fins with scissors. Remove the backbone by inserting your knife up from the belly at the base of the head, keeping your knife pressed along the spine and cutting down the fillet until you reach the tail. Make sure that you do not cut through the back (along the dorsal fin) of the fish. Repeat this procedure to separate the other fillet from the backbone. Use scissors to snip off the backbone at the base of the head and at the tail. Discard the spine and remove the pin bones from the fillets using a pair of fish tweezers. The fish should open like a book.

WHOLE ROASTED RED SNAPPER

Rare is the Filipino who shies away from the opaque gaze of a whole fish, simply cooked and elegantly served in its natural form. As with meats and poultry, fish cooked on the bone is more flavorful and juicy than a lone fillet. Preparing a whole fish may seem like a challenge when in fact it can be quite simple. Let your fishmonger do the dirty work for you by scaling and dressing the fish (removing the scales, innards, and gills) so that all it needs when you get it home is a quick rinse under cold water. This recipe highlights fresh fish with just a tickle of citrus marinade to flavor the skin and flesh. Herbal aromatics stuffed into the belly impart an additional layer of subtle perfume. Red snapper is always a showstopper, although any firm-flesh fish (such as bass, grouper, mackerel, or whitefish) will wow your guests. I usually cook this dish under the broiler but feel free to take it out to the grill during the summer.

Serves 4

4 to 5 lbs (2 to 2½ kg) whole red snapper, scaled, dressed, and fins removed

Aromatic Stuffing

3 thin slices fresh ginger, peeled
One 3-in (10-cm) piece lemongrass
3 to 4 sprigs fresh coriander leaves (cilantro)
5 toothpicks

Marinade

1 green onion (scallion), chopped
3 tablespoons lime juice
2 tablespoons soy sauce
2 tablespoons fish sauce
1 tablespoon olive oil
2 teaspoons sugar
2 teaspoons sambal ulek or chopped Thai chiles

Stuff the fish: Rinse the cleaned, dressed fish under cold water to remove the excess blood and pat dry with paper towels. Using a sharp knife, cut three parallel slashes across each side of the fish to expose the flesh. Lay slices of ginger, lemongrass, and fresh coriander leaves (cilantro) sprigs in the belly cavity and head of the fish. Skewer the belly shut with toothpicks to seal in the aromatics. Place the stuffed fish in a large baking dish so that it fits comfortably.

Marinate the fish: Whisk together the green onion (scallion), lime juice, soy sauce, fish sauce, olive oil, sugar, and sambal ulek in a small bowl. Pour over the fish, cover with plastic wrap, and refrigerate for 10 minutes. Turn the fish over and marinate the other side for 10 minutes. Discard the marinade and transfer the fish to a flat roasting rack fitted into a foil-lined roasting pan.

Broil the fish: Set the top oven rack within 6 inches of the broiler and preheat to its highest setting. Place the fish directly underneath broiler for 7 to 9 minutes per side until the fish is cooked through at the thickest part of the fillet. Lay the fish on a serving platter and remove the toothpicks. Serve the fish immediately with a dipping sauce of soy, minced garlic, and vinegar.

MAHI MAHI IN GINGER-MISO BROTH PESA NGA MAY MISU

The short title doesn't do justice to this marvelous dish layered with the bold flavors of miso and ginger. Although there are quite a few ingredients in this soup, it truly is a brilliant, one-pot meal. Instead of adding plain miso to the broth I prefer making a concentrated *miso sofrito* paste (page 21) with garlic, tomato, and caramelized onion to slather on the mahi mahi, which then flavors the soup. The addition of lycium is a deviation from any traditional recipe for *pesa* but the juicy berries add both vibrant color and sweetness to every bite without altering the integrity of the dish. Try making this soup in a pot that you can bring directly to the table, such as a cast-iron or glazed clay pot, which will keep your soup piping hot as it is served.

Serves 4

¾ lb (350 g) mahi mahi fillets (substitute any thick meaty fish such as kingfish, whitefish, cod, grouper, catfish, turbot, skate, halibut, or snapper)

¼ cup (50 g) miso sofrito (see page 21)

Broth

One 4-in (10-cm) piece lemongrass

2 teaspoons peeled and minced fresh ginger

1 cup (225 g) sliced button mushrooms

4 to 5 (approximately ½ oz/15 g) dried shiitake mushrooms

2 tablespoons lycium, dried berries

6 cups (1½ liters) Fish or Shrimp Stock (see page 14)

1 tablespoon fish sauce

1 tablespoon soy sauce

¼ teaspoon freshly ground black pepper

3 leaves Napa cabbage, chopped

1 green onion (scallion), finely chopped

Prepare the fillets: Smear the miso sofrito on one side of the mahi mahi fillets. Set the fish aside.

Make the soup: Place the lemongrass, ginger, fresh and dried mushrooms, lycium, fish or shrimp stock, fish sauce, soy sauce, and pepper in a medium soup pot (3 to 4 quarts/liters). Cover the pot and simmer the broth for 15 minutes. Remove and discard the lemongrass. Add the cabbage and the mahi mahi fillets to the pot. Cover and simmer for 5 to 7 minutes, until the mahi mahi is cooked. Ladle the soup into bowls and sprinkle with the chopped green onion (scallion).

Variation: For a vegetarian version, substitute firm tofu for the mahi mahi and vegetable stock (page 15) for the fish stock.

SWEET-AND-SOUR SKATE WING ESCABECHE NGA ISDA

Forget about any notions of sweet and sour that include thick, sticky, neon orange sauce because Filipino *escabeche* steps out of the mold. Escabeche takes its name from the Spanish verb *escabechar*, meaning "to pickle," which reflects the vibrant native vinegar used to sour the light sauce. However, vinegar is only one of several bold flavors that transform this dish into a special indulgence. The "sweet" comes naturally packaged in the form of fresh ripe pineapple and pineapple juice. Plenty of ginger and fermented black beans are the secret ingredients that help complete the alchemy. A good-quality fish or seafood stock is essential, not only for its flavor backbone but for the gelatin that will allow the sauce to reduce into shiny satin without a starch thickener. I've used many different types of fish for this escabeche and found that the delicate meat of skate pairs beautifully with the sunny flavors in this dish. Skate might require a special order from your fishmonger, but it is worth the effort.

Serves 4

1½ lbs (675 g) skate wing, skinned (substitute bass, whitefish, grouper, snapper, or tilapia)
Dash of salt and freshly ground pepper
1 cup (125 ml) all-purpose flour
2 tablespoons olive oil
2 cloves garlic, minced
2 teaspoons minced ginger
1 tablespoon fermented black beans
¼ cup (50 ml) rice wine
½ cup (125 ml) Fish Stock (see page 14)
1 cup (75 g) diced pineapple
¼ cup (50 ml) pineapple juice
1 tablespoon vinegar
1 tablespoon fish sauce
¼ teaspoon ground black pepper
1 small red bell pepper, deseeded and sliced
8 oz (225 g) Napa cabbage, finely shredded
1 green onion (scallion), sliced

Place the skate on a plate and season both sides with salt and pepper (see skate in "Buying Filipino Ingredients," page 173). Dredge the fish in the flour, shaking off any excess. Heat the oil in a large skillet over high heat. When the oil is hot and smoking, carefully add the fish without overcrowding the pan. Sear the fish for 3 to 4 minutes per side until well browned and half cooked. Remove to a plate and set aside. Remove the pan from the heat and allow it to cool slightly for 1 minute.

Lower the heat to medium. Add the garlic, ginger, and black beans to the pan. Cook and stir for 30 seconds. Deglaze the pan with the rice wine, scraping any caramelized bits into the liquid. Add the fish stock, pineapple and juice, vinegar, fish sauce, and pepper. Increase the heat to high and cook for 7 to 8 minutes to reduce the sauce and marry the flavors.

Return the fish to the pan. Top the fish with the bell pepper. Cover and simmer for 2 to 4 minutes until the fish is cooked through.

To serve, arrange the shredded cabbage on a serving platter. Lay the skate on top of the cabbage. Pour the sauce and the red bell peppers over the fish and sprinkle with the sliced green onion (scallion). Serve hot.

CABBAGE-WRAPPED TILAPIA IN COCONUT MILK   SINANGLAY

There's something nostalgic about wrapped dishes that take me back to those early Saturday mornings in the kitchen with my mom, sister, and grandmother, our culinary *kurom* (quorum), where we'd wrap enough *lumpia* egg rolls or *suman* rice cakes to feed the neighborhood. You won't need a posse or a dedicated weekend to prepare this simple wrapped fish that, with just a few ingredients, returns big flavors with interest. Tilapia is a booming business in Filipino aquaculture and my fillet of choice, but any thick, firm-fleshed whitefish will do the trick. The thin, pliable leaves of Napa cabbage perfectly cloak the tilapia without the preliminary step of blanching. I cut off the heavy white rib and use the tender leaves. For added panache, long chives tied around the wrapped fish will secure the cabbage and give this weekday dish a fancy feel.

Serves 4

1 large head Napa cabbage, approximately 1½ lbs (675 g)

3 green onions (scallions), finely chopped

2 cloves garlic, minced

1 teaspoon peeled and minced fresh ginger

1 teaspoon grated lime zest

1 teaspoon sambal ulek or chopped Thai chile

½ teaspoon olive oil

4 tilapia fillets, approximately 1½ lbs (675 g)

Salt and freshly ground black pepper to taste

8 to 10 chives, 5 to 7 in (15 to 17 cm) long

1 cup (250 ml) coconut milk

1 cup (250 ml) Fish Stock (see page 14)

2 teaspoons fish sauce

1 small bay leaf

Prepare the cabbage: Tear off 2 large cabbage leaves per fillet. Cut off the stiff white rib that runs through the center of each leaf so that you have the tender green leaves to wrap the fish. Reserve the ribs for your next soup, sauté, or stir-fry. Set the leaves aside.

Prepare the topping and wrap the fish: Combine the spring onions (scallions), garlic, ginger, lime zest, sambal ulek, and olive oil in a small bowl. Stir to mix. Lay a cabbage leaf on your work surface. Place a piece of tilapia in the center of the leaf and season with salt and pepper. Spread a teaspoon of the green onion (scallion) mixture on top of the tilapia. Wrap the cabbage around the fish so that it is completely covered. Use a second cabbage leaf if necessary. Secure the cabbage around the fish by tying a long chive around the wrapped fish like a ribbon. Continue wrapping the remaining fillets.

Cook the fish: Place the wrapped fish in a single layer in a 12-inch (30-cm) skillet. Pour in the coconut milk, fish broth, fish sauce, and bay leaf. Cover and simmer for 7 to 9 minutes until the fish is cooked through and is flaky. Remove and discard the bay leaf. Adjust the seasonings with the fish sauce and freshly ground black pepper. Transfer wrapped fish onto a serving platter and pour the sauce over the fish. Serve with Steamed Rice (page 21).

GRILLED GROUPER WITH EGGPLANT-PRUNE COMPOTE
INASAL NGA LAPU LAPU

Lapu Lapu holds an illustrious role in Filipino history as the heroic tribal chieftain who led his men into battle defending Mactan Island from the claim and colonization of Spain's hired explorer, Ferdinand Magellan. Forty-four years would pass before Spain eventually gained sovereignty over the Philippines but Lapu Lapu's undeniable heroism was never forgotten. It earned him two significant namesakes in the Philippines: Lapu Lapu City located on the island of Cebu and the prized *lapu lapu* fish that we know as grouper. The firm, sweet flesh of grouper lends itself to this flavorful miso-tomato marinade. The simplicity of the fish and the natural sweetness of the eggplant-prune compote is perfectly balanced with a side of tangy *achara,* or pickled vegetables.

Serves 4

2 lbs (900 g) grouper fillets
½ cup (125 g) miso
1½ cups (350 ml) tomato juice
1 teaspoon peeled and chopped fresh ginger
2 cloves garlic, peeled
1 green onion (scallion), coarsely chopped
1 tablespoon finely minced lemongrass
1 tablespoon fish sauce
2 tablespoons olive oil
Approximately 4 cups (600 g) Eggplant-Prune Compote (see page 20)

Marinate the fillets: Place the grouper fillets in a shallow baking dish. Combine the miso, tomato juice, ginger, garlic, green onion (scallion), lemongrass, fish sauce, and olive oil in a blender and puree until smooth. Pour over the grouper fillets and marinate in the refrigerator for 30 minutes.

Grill the fillets: Remove the fillets from the marinade, discarding any excess liquid. Preheat a stovetop grill or outdoor grill to a high flame. Lightly oil the grill and cook the fillets 4 to 6 minutes per side until just cooked.

Place on a platter and serve with hot eggplant-prune compote (page 20) and chilled achara (page 62).

RAINBOW TROUT STUFFED WITH KABOCHA SQUASH AND WATER SPINACH

I have my former sous chef, Joaquin Soler, to thank for this treasure—healthy and delicious with the whopping flavors of roasted squash and adobo-seasoned water spinach. Use a rich, flavorful fish broth to make your simple sauce really shine. Admittedly, there are a few steps to preparing these fish rolls—from roasting the squash to sautéing the *kangkong*, to rolling the trout and tying them with chives for compact elegance—so be ready to invest an hour or so in the kitchen. The final cooking time, however, is short and takes place in one pan for easy cleanup. I love serving this for formal gatherings because much of it can be prepared in advance and simply reheated before serving so that your time is better spent with your guests instead of in the kitchen.

Makes 6 rolled trout

6 rainbow trout fillets (approximately 4 oz/125 g each)
1 lb (450 g) kabocha squash (substitute butternut squash)
Salt and freshly ground black pepper to taste
1 lb (450 g) kangkong water spinach, washed
1 teaspoon olive oil
1 clove garlic, chopped
2 teaspoons soy sauce
1 teaspoon vinegar
6 long chives (at least 6 in/15 cm long)
½ cup (125 ml) rice wine
2 cups (500 ml) Fish Stock (see page 14)
2 teaspoons fish sauce
½ lb (225 g) medium-thick asparagus, ends trimmed and peeled

Prepare the trout: Preparing your trout means making sure the fillets are free from fins and bones. Use sharp kitchen shears to cut off the fins and needlenose pliers to pull out fine pinbones from the fillets. Do not remove the skin from the fillets since it helps hold the delicate flesh together. Set the cleaned fillets aside in the refrigerator until ready to use.

Roast the squash: Preheat the oven to 400°F (204°C). Cut the squash in half lengthwise. Scoop out and discard the seeds. Lay the squash cut side down on a foil-lined baking sheet and bake for 45 minutes to 1 hour until a knife easily pierces the tender flesh. Once cool, scrape the flesh into a bowl and mash with a fork. Season with salt and pepper.

Prepare the water spinach: Rinse the kangkong well and shake off the excess water. Separate the leaves from the stems. Cut the stems into ½-inch (1¼-cm) pieces. Heat the olive oil in a large 3 to 4 quarts/liters sauté pan over medium heat. Add the garlic and cook for 30 seconds being careful not to burn it. Add the kangkong stems and sauté for 5 to 7 minutes until softened. Add the kangkong leaves, soy sauce, vinegar, and pepper and cook for another 5 minutes until wilted. Remove the sautéed kangkong to a bowl and cool. Wash your sauté pan and return it to the stove for later use.

Stuff the trout: Lay a trout fillet on your work surface, skin side down. Season the fish with salt and pepper. Spread 1 to 2 tablespoons mashed squash on the trout, leaving a ¼-inch (6½-mm) border of fillet uncovered by the squash. Lay 1 to 2 tablespoons sautéed kangkong on top of the squash. Starting at the tail, roll up the trout and secure it closed by tying a chive around the roll. In a pinch, you can seal the trout fillet closed using toothpicks or skewers, which will make searing the fish more cumbersome. Continue rolling and tying the remaining fillets.

Braise the trout: Heat the sauté pan with olive oil over high heat. When the oil is smoking, add the trout rolls to the pan, skin side down. Sear each side of the rolls for 1 to 2 minutes until well browned. Once seared, lay the rolls upright and add the rice wine, fish broth, and fish sauce to the pan. Cover and cook for 8 to 10 minutes until the fish is completely cooked through. Remove the fish rolls to a serving platter and keep warm. Add the asparagus to the pan and cover. Cook the asparagus for 4 to 5 minutes until crisp-tender. Place on the platter with the trout rolls. Continue cooking sauce for another 2 to 3 minutes until the broth is reduced. Adjust the seasonings and pour over the fish rolls. Serve immediately.

BATTERED FRIED SHRIMP HIPON REBOSADO

Every family has its own food traditions, special dishes that punctuate festive gatherings and celebrations. In my family, a heaping platter of shrimp *rebosado* on the table is love incarnate and a sure sign of the cook's affection. Rebosado isn't the typical fiesta dish, long and involved with a ticker-tape list of ingredients. It's a flash to prepare with ingredients that you most likely already have in your cupboard. What makes it special is the shrimp: the largest, meatiest shrimp you can find. This recipe calls for jumbo (11–15) black tiger shrimp, meaning there are 11 to 15 shrimp per pound. Have plenty of Sweet Chili Sauce for dunking.

Makes 11–15 shrimp
1 lb (450 g) jumbo black tiger shrimp, peeled with tails left on and deveined
1 tablespoon oyster sauce
1 tablespoon soy sauce
Pinch of freshly ground black pepper

Batter
½ cup (75 g) all-purpose flour
½ cup (70 g) cornstarch
1 large egg
¾ cup (175 ml) milk
2 to 3 cups (500 to 750 ml) oil, for frying

In a bowl, combine the shrimp with the oyster sauce, soy sauce, and pepper. Mix thoroughly and set aside. In another bowl, whisk together the batter ingredients until smooth.

Heat the oil in a medium pot to 350°F (175°C). Take a shrimp by the tail and dip it into the batter coating it evenly. Gently place the shrimp into the oil and fry for 3 to 5 minutes until golden brown. Dry the shrimp on paper towels. Serve immediately with sweet chili sauce (page 18).

CRAB AND EGGPLANT TORTE TORTANG ALAMANG

One of the classic recipes in my mother's large repertoire of amazing dishes is this crab and eggplant torta, heavily seasoned with garlic and oyster sauce and slowly cooked with egg. It's not much to look at, but the flavor is break-your-heart good. Use good-quality lump crabmeat with large chunks of crab instead of cheaper crab flakes that will ruin the smooth texture of this dish. For years I had always roasted my eggplant in the oven, when my mom let me in on her quick-cooking secret: using the microwave! It works beautifully, cooking the eggplant in a fraction of the time while keeping it moist and tender. This has always been a stovetop dish for my mom, using her trusty nonstick pan and lots of oil to keep the eggs from sticking. To eliminate much of the oil, I've switched to baking this torta in the oven with stellar results—even by Mom's standards.

Serves 4

1 eggplant, approximately 1 lb (450 g)
¼ cup (50 ml) oyster sauce
2 teaspoons soy sauce
¼ teaspoon freshly ground black pepper
7 large eggs, beaten
2 green onions (scallions), chopped
2 cloves garlic, chopped
1 teaspoon minced ginger
1 lb (450 g) lump crabmeat

Cook the eggplant: To cook the egg-plant in a microwave, follow Step 1; to cook it in a conventional oven, fol-low Step 2. **Step 1.** Pierce the egg-plant in several places with a knife and place on a microwavable dish. Cook on high for 9 to 15 minutes until completely cooked and very tender. **Step 2.** To cook the eggplant in a conventional oven, first pierce the eggplant skin with a knife in sev-eral places. Place the whole eggplant on a baking sheet. Cook in a 375°F (190°C) preheated oven for 45 min-utes to 1 hour until very tender and ready to collapse.

Prepare and cook the torte: Cool the eggplant and remove the stem and skin. Finely chop the eggplant and place in a large bowl. Add the oyster sauce, soy sauce, pepper, eggs, spring onions (scallions), garlic, and ginger. Mix well to combine. Fold the crabmeat into the egg mixture, being careful not to break apart the large chunks of crab.

Preheat the oven to 375°F (190°C). Pour the crab mixture into a lightly oiled 9 by 13-inch (23 by 33-m) bak-ing dish and bake for 45 minutes to 1 hour until the mixture is firmly set. Serve hot with rice.

GREEN LIP MUSSELS WITH MISO GUISADONG TAHONG NGA MAY MISU

Whenever I'm pressed for time, mussels often come to mind as the solution to my dinner dilemma. Healthy and delicious, mussels need little preparation and almost no cooking time so that dinner can be on the table from start to finish in less than 30 minutes. Paired with a comfortable, almost drinkable sauce transformed by the warmth of miso and richness of coconut milk, this dish will surely become a weekday staple. For this recipe I prefer using large, succulent green lip mussels that are abundantly fresh in the Philippines, although rarely available fresh in the States for home consumption. Excellent quality New Zealand green lip mussels are available on the half-shell in the grocer's frozen seafood section. Fresh black mussels, which most large grocery stores stock fresh, are equally delicious.

Serves 4

1 tablespoon olive oil
1 small onion, chopped
2 cloves garlic, chopped
1 teaspoon peeled and minced fresh
  ginger
1 tomato, diced
2 tablespoons miso
1 cup (250 ml) Fish Stock (see
  page 14)
¼ cup (50 ml) coconut milk
½ teaspoon fish sauce
1 teaspoon shrimp paste
¼ teaspoon freshly ground black
  pepper
2 lbs (900 g) frozen green lip mussels on the half-shell, thawed
¼ cup (10 g) chopped fresh coriander leaves (cilantro)

Heat the olive oil in a large sauté pan (4 to 5 quarts/liters) over medium heat. Add the onion, garlic, and ginger. Cook and stir for 2 minutes, until onion is translucent. Add the tomato and miso. Cook and stir for 5 to 6 minutes; the tomato will collapse and blend easily into the miso paste.

Add the fish stock, coconut milk, fish sauce, shrimp paste, pepper, and mussels. Cover and simmer for 5 to 7 minutes, until the mussels are heated through. Stir in the fresh coriander leaves (cilantro). Ladle the mussels and sauce into a serving dish. Serve with rice or bread.

WATER SPINACH ADOBO ADOBONG KANGKONG

SWEET POTATOES, PLANTAINS, AND JACKFRUIT IN

COCONUT SAUCE GUINATAAN

COCONUT CORN PUDDING MAJA BLANCA MAIS

STEWED SQUASH, EGGPLANT, AND LONG BEANS PINAKBET

COCONUT-GARLIC MASHED POTATOES

CHAYOTE WITH MUSHROOMS AND WATERCRESS

STUFFED EGGPLANT WITH CURRY-TOMATO SOFRITO RELLENONG TALONG

HOISIN-TAMARIND GLAZED LONG BEANS GUISADONG SITAO

VEGETABLES

When I think of Filipino food, vegetables don't immediately come to the forefront of my mind. Certainly, that's not to say that there isn't an ample selection of vegetables to accompany any Filipino meal. The Philippines is a veritable wonderland of tropical vegetation, where fruits of the soil are abundant and available to the local population. But let's face it. In a predominantly rural, developing country, vegetarianism is more a forced condition than one of choice. As such, protein-based foods hold more value in the Filipino diet than vegetables alone; so vegetable dishes, though fundamental in a Filipino meal, are rarely vegetarian. More common are vegetables flavored with some type of seafood, poultry, or meat—appealing to the economy of a single dish—which make a complete meal when eaten with rice.

This chapter features vegetables in varying forms and functions. *Pinakbet*, a national dish of lightly stewed vegetables flavored with fermented shrimp paste, incorporates beautiful patty pan squash available during Chicago's short summer. However, a simple substitution of kabocha or butternut squash for patty pans will give you a more traditional version and allow you to enjoy the bounty of fall and winter. Potatoes are one of my favorite vegetables, versatile as both a starch and vegetable. Though potatoes could never replace rice as the primary starch in the Philippines, I would feel remiss as an American not to include some form of potatoes in this collection. That's where the Coconut-Garlic Mashed Potatoes come in, a rich, aromatic, and fantastic way to dress up an American favorite. Filipino *saba*, a cooking banana, is frequently used both as a savory and sweet ingredient in our cuisine. Here I've featured an easy-to-find substitute, the plantain, in *Guinataan*, a stew of banana, sweet potatoes, summer squash, and a hint of tropical sweetness added with coconut milk and the unique flavor of jackfruit.

The *Adobong Kangkong* is one of my favorites served hot or cold. *Kangkong*, or water spinach, is outstanding not so much for its leaves, which are similar to that of regular spinach, but for its hollow stems that retain a snazzy textural crunch even after sautéing.

If you've never tried chayote, Chayote with Mushrooms and Watercress will turn you on to this delicious and versatile squash common in most grocery stores. I've paired chayote with a double dose of shiitake mushrooms (fresh and dried) and peppery watercress for an addictive side dish that is a wonderful alternative to zucchini or yellow squash. Because Chinese long beans have always been a vegetable essential in my family, being an easy and prolific grower in the garden, I usually have a greater supply of beans than I have ways of cooking them. I stick to the basics when cooking beans, doing a quick sauté with butter and garlic or spicing it up with the Hoisin-Tamarind Glaze (page 145). I guarantee, this glaze will become a staple in your refrigerator. Dab a little on your sautéed broccoli, asparagus, or carrots; baste it on your grilled meats and chicken; use it as a dipping sauce for pot stickers or egg rolls. It's that good.

WATER SPINACH ADOBO ADOBONG KANGKONG

Water spinach, or *kangkong* is pretty easy to pick out in the Asian greens aisle, which can carry nearly as intimidating a selection as the noodle aisle. With long, skinny, arrow-shaped leaves densely shooting up around willowy, hollow stems, kangkong is the giraffe among the horses, so to speak, and more than likely the longest of Asian greens. The tender leaves are very similar in flavor to spinach when cooked, although kangkong's mouthfeel has a light slickness that I prefer over spinach's astringency. The hollow stems, on the other hand, are outstanding because of their crisp firm texture that contrasts wonderfully against the wilted leaves. What I love about this dish (besides the kangkong) is that it is just as delicious served hot off the stove as it is served chilled from the refrigerator humbly garnished with sliced tomato, shaved red onion, or cucumber.

Serves 4 as a side dish

1 lb (450 g) kangkong water
    spinach, leaves and stems
1 tablespoon olive oil
2 cloves garlic, chopped
1 green onion (scallion), chopped
½ teaspoon peeled and minced fresh
    ginger
¾ cup (175 ml) Vegetable or Chicken
    Stock (see page 15)
1½ teaspoons soy sauce
1 teaspoon fish sauce
1 teaspoon coconut or palm vinegar
1 small bay leaf
¼ teaspoon freshly ground black
    pepper

Prepare the kangkong: Clean the kangkong by rinsing the leaves and stems under cold water and drying them on a kitchen towel. Pick the leaves off the stems and cut the stems into 2-inch (5-cm) pieces. Set the leaves and stems aside in separate bowls.

Sauté the kangkong: Heat the olive oil in a large 12 to 14-inch sauté pan or skillet over medium heat. Sauté the garlic, green onion (scallion), and ginger for 30 seconds. Add the kangkong stems and sauté for another 2 minutes. Add the kangkong leaves, vegetable or chicken stock, soy sauce, fish sauce, vinegar, bay leaf, and pepper. Cover and steam for 7 to 9 minutes. Remove the cover and toss to combine. Discard the bay leaf and serve hot.

SWEET POTATOES, PLANTAINS, AND JACKFRUIT IN COCONUT SAUCE
GUINATAAN

Traditionally, this dish is more of a dessert soup using savory ingredients such as *saba* (the native Filipino cooking banana), sweet potato, taro root, and plenty of coconut milk. Without the incomparable flavor of coconut milk, the dish just isn't the same. But this healthier alternative turns the soup into a vegetable side dish that maintains the original's flavor, using just a hint of coconut milk. Though saba bananas are difficult to find in the States, plantains are an excellent substitute. I also love serving this dish during the summer, which allows me to use the freshest corn along with *lanka*, or jackfruit. Jackfruit is a tropical fruit, popular in Filipino cuisine for its very distinct flavor that complements both savory and sweet dishes. I am often asked for a suitable substitute, but, unfortunately, I haven't yet found one with similar flavor. Jackfruit comes in a couple of preserved forms—either canned in a light syrup or frozen. Once in awhile, I'll be lucky enough to find it fresh at the Asian grocer either whole or precut into sections.

Serves 6

1 tablespoon olive oil
1 green onion (scallion), thinly sliced
2 cloves garlic, chopped
1 teaspoon peeled and minced fresh ginger
1 sweet potato, cut into ½-in (1⅓-cm) cubes
1 firm ripe plantain (approximately 10 oz/280 g), cut into ½-in (1⅓-cm) cubes
¼ cup (50 ml) Vegetable or Chicken Stock (see page 15)

¼ cup (50 ml) coconut milk
½ cup (75 g) sliced jackfruit
¼ lb (125 g) zucchini, cut into ½-in (1⅓-cm) cubes
¼ lb (125 g) yellow squash, cut into ½-in (1⅓-cm) cubes
2 ears corn, grilled with kernels cut from the cob
1 tablespoon soy sauce

Heat the olive oil in a large pot over medium heat. Add the green onion (scallion), garlic, and ginger. Cook and stir for 30 seconds. Add the sweet potato, plantain, vegetable or chicken stock, coconut milk, and jackfruit. Cover and simmer for 15 to 20 minutes until the sweet potatoes become tender.

Add the zucchini, yellow squash, corn, and soy sauce and simmer for another 5 to 7 minutes until the summer squash is tender and the coconut milk has thickened into a rich sauce. Ladle onto a platter and serve hot.

COCONUT CORN PUDDING MAJA BLANCA MAIS

Maja blanca mais is a Filipino dessert or snack, a firm pudding flavored with coconut milk and corn and thickened on the stovetop with cornstarch. It is a delicious combination of flavors that I wanted to bring to the dinner table as an accompaniment to meats instead of rice. This recipe takes the essential ingredients and flavors of a traditional maja blanca mais and, with just a few minor adjustments to proportions, transforms it into a creamy, savory side dish, similar in texture to Italian polenta. It pairs magnificently with hearty stewed dishes such as Humba (page 108), Caldereta (page 108), and meat stir-fries, such as the Corriander-Crusted Beef (page 110) or Bistek (page 112).

Serves 4

1 (13½-oz/400-ml) can coconut milk
1½ cups (375 ml) water
¼ cup (50 g) sugar
¾ cup (125 g) yellow cornmeal
2 tablespoons glutinous rice flour
½ teaspoon salt
Dash of freshly ground black pepper
½ cup (75 g) corn kernels
½ cup (125 g) sour cream

Combine the coconut milk, water, sugar, cornmeal, rice flour, salt, pepper, and corn kernels in a large pot. Bring the mixture to a simmer over low-medium heat for 10 to 15 minutes, stirring frequently with a spoon or spatula to prevent the bottom from burning. It will become thick and creamy. Remove from the heat and stir in the sour cream until well combined. Serve hot.

STEWED SQUASH, EGGPLANT, AND LONG BEANS PINAKBET

I've enjoyed *pinakbet*, a stewed vegetable medley, in many forms ranging from a saucy, tomato-laden stew to a dry sauté with the barest hint of tomato sofrito. Often a subtle meat or seafood element such as sliced pork, *chorizo de Bilbao*, or shrimp is added to complement the vegetables without overshadowing their freshness. But what every pinakbet has in common is shrimp paste, called *bagoong hipon* or *bagoong alamang*, the popular pungent condiment that when added to a dish lets you know that you're not in Kansas anymore. I make my own version of *bagoong* for this recipe by sautéing a paste of tiny dried shrimp and fish sauce together with garlic and tomato to provide just the slightest hint of the sea. The vegetables are the focus of this year-round specialty. Butternut or kabocha squash swaps for pattypan during the cold months.

Serves 4

Shrimp Paste
1 tablespoon olive oil
1 heaping teaspoon dried shrimp
1 clove garlic, peeled
2 teaspoons fish sauce

Pinakbet
2 tablespoons olive oil
1 small onion, chopped
1 teaspoon peeled and minced fresh
　ginger
1 small tomato, diced
1 tablespoon tomato paste
2 tablespoons rice wine
½ cup (125 ml) Shrimp or Chicken
　Stock (see pages 14 and 15)
¼ lb (125 g) Chinese long beans, cut
　into 2-in (5-cm) pieces
¼ lb (125 g) round Thai eggplant,
　quartered (substitute any eggplant
　variety)
¼ lb (125 g) pattypan squash,
　quartered
¼ teaspoon freshly ground black
　pepper

Make the shrimp paste: Use a mortar and pestle to mash together the olive oil, dried shrimp, garlic, and fish sauce until it forms a paste. Set aside. You may also substitute ½ teaspoon jarred bagoong alamang shrimp paste instead of making your own.

Cook the vegetables: Heat the olive oil in a large skillet over medium heat. When the oil is moderately hot add the onion, ginger, and tomato. Cook and stir for 1 minute until the onion becomes translucent. Add the shrimp paste, tomato paste, rice wine, and the shrimp or chicken stock. Simmer the mixture for 5 minutes, stirring occasionally. Add the beans, eggplant, and squash. Season with black pepper. Cover and simmer for 10 to 15 minutes until the vegetables are tender when pierced with a fork. Serve hot.

COCONUT-GARLIC MASHED POTATOES

I could hardly consider myself an American without admitting my addiction to mashed potatoes, the ultimate in American comfort food. However, the Filipina in me often requires that even the most American dishes have elements of Filipino flavor. Coconut milk and garlic don't make these potatoes lighter or fluffier, healthier, or easier to prepare. Coconut milk and garlic just make them taste better, plain and simple.

Serves 6

2½ lbs (900 g) Yukon gold potatoes, peeled and cut into 1-in (2½-cm) cubes
8 cloves garlic, peeled
1 small bay leaf
5 to 6 cups (1 to 1½ liters) water
1 (12½ oz) can coconut milk
2 tablespoons unsalted butter
1½ teaspoons salt
¼ teaspoon freshly ground black pepper

Place the potatoes, garlic, bay leaf, and water in a large pot. There should be enough water to cover the potatoes. Bring the pot to a boil and cook for 20 to 30 minutes until the potatoes and garlic are very tender when pierced with a fork. Pour the potatoes into a strainer to drain completely. Discard the bay leaf.

Pass the potatoes and garlic through a food mill returning the mixture into the pot. Over medium heat, add the coconut milk, butter, salt, and pepper to the potatoes, folding all the ingredients together so that they are well blended. Cook 3 to 4 minutes until the butter has melted and the potatoes are hot.

CHAYOTE WITH MUSHROOMS AND WATERCRESS

It's very easy to pass right over chayote in the produce section, where it is often nestled off to the side of its more recognizable squash relatives. Filipinos have the Spaniards to thank for importing this Mexican native onto their soil. Chayote is a low-maintenance, versatile vegetable that is crisp and mild when eaten raw and delicately tender when cooked. Like zucchini or yellow summer squash, chayote has nice texture but it tends to lean toward blandness, which is why I find it best featured in boldly flavored soups, stews, or stir-fries. Here the chayote, shown to the right, is highlighted with mushrooms, both fresh and dried, for a double dose of earthiness and tossed with peppery watercress for a snappy finish.

Serves 4

¼ cup (50 ml) rice wine
¼ cup (50 ml) hot water
3 to 4 dried shiitake mushrooms
1 teaspoon olive oil
2 cloves garlic, chopped
1 green onion (scallion), chopped
1 chayote, cubed
¼ lb (125 g) fresh shiitake mushrooms, stems removed
1 tablespoon soy sauce
1 teaspoon fish sauce
¼ teaspoon ground black pepper
2 bunches watercress, rinsed with woody stems removed
1 lime, sliced into wedges

Combine the rice wine and hot water in a bowl. Soak the dried mushrooms in the liquid for 15 minutes until tender. Remove the mushrooms, squeezing excess liquid back into the bowl. Remove the woody stems with scissors or a sharp knife. Slice the mushroom caps thinly and set aside. Reserve the soaking liquid.

Heat the olive oil in a medium sauté pan (2 to 3 quarts/liters) over medium heat. Add the garlic and green onion (scallion) to the pan.

Cook and stir for 15 seconds, being careful not to burn the garlic. Add the diced chayote, the mushroom soaking liquid, the reconstituted mushrooms, button mushrooms, soy sauce, fish sauce, and pepper. Cover and cook for 7 to 10 minutes until the chayote is tender. Toss in the watercress and return the cover to the pan, allowing the watercress to steam for 1 minute. Pour the vegetables onto a serving platter and garnish with lime wedges. Serve hot.

STUFFED EGGPLANT WITH CURRY-TOMATO SOFRITO
RELLENONG TALONG

There is a flavor interplay between three components in this dish that makes it outstanding: caramelized onions, chorizo de Bilbao, and curry-tomato sofrito. The curry-tomato confit is an essential condiment in my refrigerator that I often use in place of a basic sofrito to excite my stews, sautés, or stir-fries. Naturally, fresh curry paste tastes better than dried curry powder. If an Indian market or Asian grocer is not close by, try experimenting with your own home-made curry paste, using ingredients that you love. I guarantee that once you've found the perfect combination of fresh chiles, lemongrass, ginger, and spices, powdered curry will never find a place in your kitchen again.

Serves 4

2 lbs (900 g) Chinese or Japanese eggplant
2 cloves garlic, chopped
1 tablespoon soy sauce
2 tablespoons oyster sauce
¼ teaspoon freshly ground black pepper
3 large eggs, beaten
1 tablespoon unsalted butter
1 onion, diced
¼ cup (50 ml) rice wine

¼ lb (125 g) chorizo de Bilbao or Chinese sausage, diced
1 cup (250 ml) Curry-Tomato Sofrito (see page 17)
1 green onion (scallion), thinly sliced on a bias

Cook the eggplant: To cook the eggplant in a microwave, follow Step 1; to cook it in a conventional oven, follow Step 2. **Step 1.** Cut the eggplant in half lengthwise and place on a microwaveable dish. Cook on high for 9 to 12 minutes until the eggplant flesh is very tender in the center when pierced with a skewer. Remove from the microwave and set aside to cool. **Step 2.** To cook the eggplant in a conventional oven, first pierce the eggplant skin with a knife in several places. Place the whole eggplant on a baking sheet. Cook in a 375°F (190°C) preheated oven for 45 minutes to 1 hour until very tender and ready to collapse. Remove from the oven and set aside to cool.

Prepare the eggplant filling: Use a spoon to gently scrape out the tender flesh into a bowl, being careful not to tear the skin. Reserve the skins.

Combine the cooked eggplant, garlic, soy sauce, oyster sauce, pepper, and eggs in a bowl and mix well. Set aside.

Cook the eggplant filling: Preheat the oven to 350°F (175°C). Melt the butter in a large ovenproof skillet over medium heat. Add the onion and cook for 7 to 10 minutes, stirring occasionally, until the onion caramelizes evenly to a golden brown. Deglaze the pan with the rice wine, scraping off any caramelized onion bits into the pan. Add the chorizo and cook for another minute. Pour the eggplant mixture into the pan and cook, without stirring, over medium heat for 3 to 5 minutes until the eggs begin to set. Transfer the skillet from the stove to the oven and bake the eggplant for 25 to 30 minutes until the eggs have fully set. Remove the eggplant from the oven and cool slightly before stuffing the skins.

Stuff the eggplant skins: Spoon the cooked eggplant into the skins. Spread warm curry-tomato sofrito on top and garnish with a sprinkle of green onion (scallion). Serve immediately while hot.

You can prepare this dish a day ahead and reheat the eggplant in a preheated 350°F (175°C) oven.

HOISIN-TAMARIND GLAZED LONG BEANS   GUISADONG SITAO

Guisado means "stew" and *sitao* are Chinese long beans. The intimidating bundles of 1 to 3-foot-long beans may look unapproachable coiled up on the grocer's stand. But if you've purchased and cooked American varieties of green beans, you already know what to do with these beauties. Look for beans that are pencil-thin and approximately 1 to 1½ feet (30 to 46 cm) in length. At this stage they will be at their peak of tenderness. Longer thicker beans are older and tend to become tough with age. Long beans are either pale or dark green in color and should be free of brown spots or discolorations. Although long beans have bumpy textured skin, the pliant beans should never be withered or limp. Cut the beans into 2 to 3-inch pieces and cook them as you would any American variety. The hoisin-tamarind sauce used to flavor these beans is an explosion of sweet and tangy that you won't soon forget. It also makes a handy glaze for your steamed or stir-fried vegetables. Try it on broccoli, asparagus, cauliflower, or carrots.

Serves 4

Hoisin-Tamarind Glaze: makes 1 cup (250 ml)
1 teaspoon olive oil
1 clove garlic, minced
1 teaspoon peeled and minced fresh ginger
1 teaspoon sambal ulek or dried red pepper flakes
½ cup (125 ml) tamarind juice
½ cup (125 ml) hoisin sauce

Glazed Long Beans
1 tablespoon grapeseed oil
1½ lbs (675 g) Chinese long beans, cut into 2-in (5-cm) pieces
2 cloves garlic, chopped
3 tablespoons rice wine
¼ cup (50 ml) Vegetable or Chicken Stock (see page 15)
¼ cup (50 ml) hoisin-tamarind glaze
1 teaspoon toasted sesame seeds or
1 green onion (scallion), chopped

Make the hoisin-tamarind glaze: Heat the olive oil in a small skillet over medium heat. Sauté the garlic, ginger, and sambal ulek together for 30 seconds, being careful not to burn the garlic. Remove from the heat. Add the tamarind juice and hoisin sauce. Stir to mix well and cool. Store in an airtight container in the refrigerator for up to 2 weeks.

Cook the beans: Heat the oil in a large sauté pan or wok over high heat. When hot but not smoking add the long beans. Cook and stir for 2 to 3 minutes until the beans have started to brown. Add the garlic and cook for another minute. Add the rice wine, chicken stock, and hoisin-tamarind glaze. Cook over medium-high heat for 5 to 7 minutes until beans are fully cooked and the sauce has thickened into a glaze. Spoon the beans onto a platter and garnish with toasted sesame seeds or chopped green onion (scallion). Serve immediately.

PINEAPPLE AND CASSAVA TARTS

ALMOND LECHE FLAN

FILIPINO FRUIT SUNDAE HALO-HALO

TEA CUSTARD EARL GRAY NATILLAS

MERINGUE ROLL WITH CHOCOLATE CREAM CHOCOLATE BRAZO DE MERCEDES

CASHEW TORTE WITH VANILLA MOUSSE SANS RIVAL

COCONUT-PANDAN TAPIOCA BUKO PANDAN SAGO

AMBROSIA SHORTCAKE WITH CASSAVA BISCUIT

BANANA, CHOCOLATE, AND COCONUT EGG ROLLS TURON

DESSERTS

I love desserts—rich buttery cakes piled high with frosting, fruit pies with flaky crusts, smooth creamy custards, gooey puddings, and chocolate in any incarnation. However, Asian desserts generally follow a different philosophy from the European confections that excite my sweet tooth. Undressed fresh fruits are always a welcome, delicious end to an Asian meal, highlighting nature's simplicity. Along the same lines, fruits and even vegetables (namely yams, mung beans, or corn) are sweetened with a sugary syrup and lightly flavored with ginger or citrus peel to make a unique dessert soup. Steamed cakes thickened with tapioca starch or glutinous rice flour are more the standard than oven-baked, egg-leavened cakes. Stovetop puddings are also a common favorite with tapioca pearls and rice heading the top of the list.

Fortunately, with Filipino cuisine, you don't have to decide between the European and Asian dessert philosophy since they are both incorporated into everyday sweets. Naturally, geography has determined popular ingredients used for desserts. Coconut plays an essential role as in the Buko Pandan Sago, a nostalgic yet satisfying dessert of tapioca pudding, lightly scented with fragrant pandan leaves and coconut milk for a classic flavor combination. Caramelized mangoes crown the tapioca for a tropical flourish. Cassava's starchy root is also featured here, grated and used as an alternative to wheat flour in the Pineapple and Cassava Tarts and the Ambrosia Shortcake with Cassava Biscuit, a Filipino interpretation of an American classic.

The Spaniards are responsible for integrating buttery cakes and eggy custards into Filipino cuisine. *Almond Leche Flan*, a fiesta staple, is made even richer than the original Spanish version by using egg yolks instead of whole eggs. The addition of condensed and evaporated milks gives our flan a distinctive "Filipinoness" that sets it apart from Spanish or Mexican flan. Natilla is a baked custard very similar to French crème brûlée, although it typically does not have a burnt sugar crust. I've lightly scented my *natilla* with the flavor of Earl Gray tea, a delicious pairing with custard.

Cakes in this chapter are abundant. The Chocolate Brazo de Mercedes is a lighter version of the American jelly roll. Instead of a traditional *ube* (sweetened purple yam) filling, I've dusted the meringue cake with cocoa powder and wrapped it around chocolate cream. Because there is nothing more perfect than a light dessert to enjoy at summer cookouts, I've also included multiple Brazo variations, using lemon, mocha, and pumpkin. Sans Rival, a showstopping rectangular torte of vanilla cream layered in between cashew meringue cake cloaked in chocolate ganache, is an extravagant treat that your family and friends won't soon forget.

I've strayed from tradition here, by highlighting desserts suited more for after-dinner enjoyment. Small finger sweets such as powdered rice candies (*polovones*), almond or peanut candies (*pastillas*), and rice cakes (*cuchinta* or *bibinka*), although common confections, are often taken as snacks during *merienda* but are not necessarily appropriate dessert fare the way Westerners think of dessert. Luckily, there are many traditional Filipino desserts that make an easy transition to the dinner table. Turon, fried fruit egg rolls, are filled with bananas, chocolate, and *macapuno* (preserved coconut). These treats are as quick to prepare as they are to cook. They're also an invaluable asset in my freezer for the unexpected guest or a midnight craving. Halo-Halo, probably the most native of our traditional desserts, is a summertime pleasure that goes beyond ice cream, sundaes, or milk shakes. Meaning "mix-mix," *halo-halo* is a combination of fresh and preserved fruits, shaved ice, ice cream, and evaporated milk that is best eaten with both a spoon and straw.

PINEAPPLE AND CASSAVA TARTS

In addition to being an excellent cook, my mother is an accomplished baker. Her cassava cake is a family institution guaranteed to convert dessert skeptics into devotees. My rendition of cassava cake admits to being a restaurant-friendly replica with unpretentious adornments worthy of the homey original. In tart form, these minicakes sandwich cassava batter in between a light puff pastry crust and a juicy caramelized pineapple. Serve the tarts lightly warmed with a scoop of vanilla ice cream for added pleasure.

Makes 6 tarts

2 lbs (900 g) store-bought puff pastry dough, thawed

Cassava Cake

1 (8-oz/225-g) package grated cassava
2½ cups (625 ml) milk
1 (14-oz) can sweetened condensed milk
¼ cup (50 g) granulated sugar
3 large eggs
1½ sticks (170 g) butter, melted

Pineapple Topping

1 ripe pineapple, peeled, cored, and sliced into ½-in (6-mm) thick rings
½ cup (100 g) brown sugar
3 tablespoons water
½ teaspoon vanilla extract

Preheat the oven to 350°F (175°C). Lightly spray 6 (4-inch/10-cm) mini-tart pans, with removable bottoms, with oil or pan spray. Unfold the thawed puff pastry dough and cut out six circles, roughly 6 inches (15 cm) in diameter. Press the dough circles into the tart pans and refrigerate until ready to fill.

Combine the cassava, milk, condensed milk, sugar, eggs, and melted butter in a mixing bowl and whisk together. Place the tart pans on a baking sheet. Ladle the tart pans with the cassava batter, leaving ½-inch border from the top rim of the tart. Bake for 25 minutes until the batter begins to set.

Remove the tarts from the oven and lay a pineapple ring in the center of each tart. Mix together the brown sugar, water, and vanilla in a small bowl. Brush the sugar mixture on top of each pineapple and return the tarts to the oven. Bake for another 20 to 30 minutes until the batter is set and the pineapple is golden brown.

Once you've removed the tarts from the oven, let them cool for 10 minutes before unmolding. Serve with a small scoop of vanilla ice cream.

ALMOND LECHE FLAN

There's a quiet elegance to a well-made flan that belies the recipe's simplicity. Perhaps it's the dark shiny caramel melted into a sweet sauce, or the creamy custard with just the right balance of eggs and milk that makes the flan rich yet light, or the perfectly smooth texture without an air bubble in sight to mar the silkiness. Leche flan is a fiesta favorite often served in a large mold well suited for the buffet table. For a no-fuss, make-ahead dessert that is sure to impress, I often serve flan individually, baked in ovenproof coffee cups or ramekins.

Makes six 4-oz (125 ml) flans
Caramel
1 cup (200 g) sugar

Flan
1 (12-oz/360-ml) can evaporated milk
½ cup sweetened condensed milk, approximately half of a 14-oz/420-g can
6 large egg yolks
½ cup (125 ml) half-and-half
1 teaspoon almond extract

Make the caramel: Place the sugar in a very clean, heavy-bottomed saucepan and cook over medium heat for 8 to 12 minutes. As the sugar melts, use a very clean pastry brush dipped in water to brush down any sugar that bubbles up the inside of the pan. Pour the caramel into six 4-ounce (125-ml) ovenproof ramekins, making sure that it covers the entire bottom. Set the molds aside and let the caramel cool completely for 15 to 20 minutes. Soak the saucepan and wooden spoon in water to dissolve the caramel for easy cleaning.

Make the flan: Combine the evaporated milk, condensed milk, egg yolks, half-and-half, and almond extract into a large bowl. Stir with a whisk, being careful not to incorporate air into the mixture. Place a fine-mesh strainer over another bowl and pour the flan through. Pour the flan into ramekins over the cooled caramel.

Cook the flan: Preheat the oven to 350°F (175°C). Place the ramekins in a large, high-sided baking dish. Pour hot tap water into the larger dish so that it reaches halfway up the sides of the ramekins. Bake the flan in the water bath loosely covered with aluminum foil for 40 to 50 minutes. The flan is ready when the surface is set but has a slight jiggle when you tap the ramekins. Remove the water bath from the oven. Remove the ramekins from the water and cool to room temperature. Cover with plastic wrap and refrigerate overnight. Flan is best served after 24 hours when the caramel has had ample time to dissolve and the custard is completely cool and set.

Unmold the flan: Run a knife around the inside of the ramekins, separating the flan from the mold. Place an individual serving plate over the flan and invert onto the plate. Pour any dissolved caramel onto the flan and serve.

Variation: Fiesta Style Flan. To make 1 large flan, follow the caramel recipe as directed above and pour into a 10-inch-round or 9-inch (22-cm)-square baking dish. Double the flan recipe and bake in a 325°F (160°C) preheated oven in a water bath loosely covered with aluminum foil for 60 to 70 minutes until the flan is set in the center. Cool, refrigerate, and unmold the flan as directed.

If there is such a thing as a national dessert of the Philippines, *halo-halo* proudly holds the title. Meaning "mix-mix," this multilayered dessert is a sundae-milk shake-slushy hybrid that's sure to quell summer's simmering heat. Halo-halo features an assortment of tropical fruits and sweetmeats chilled with shaved ice, ice cream, and evaporated milk. As the name indicates, halo-halo ingredients are a mélange of flavors and textures ranging from fresh bananas to sweet corn to preserved delicacies such as coconut gel (*nata de coco*), purple yam paste (*ube*), and sweetened kidney beans. Master halo-halo makers even go so far as to include flan custard, agar-agar, puffed rice (*pinipig*), or garbanzo beans. Perhaps it's my Western upbringing, but I've always preferred more fruit in my halo-halo than anything else, which is why this recipe is subjectively fruit-sided. The signature flavor of jackfruit is fundamental as are the chewy strands of coconut sport (a variety of the coconut palm plant), which you'll find jarred under the name *macapuno*.

One of the keys to an authentic halo-halo is shaved ice. Though crushing ice in a blender may seem like a viable alternative, a blender can't process ice into the fine flakes that make halo-halo unique. Since shaved ice drinks and desserts are popular throughout Asia, you'll be sure to find either an electric or manual ice shaver at an Asian grocer. They are also available at large chain stores that sell kitchen goods.

Serves 4
3 cups (300 g) shaved ice
1 cup (170 g) diced mango
1 cup (175 g) diced pineapple
1 cup (150 g) diced jackfruit, with
   juice
1 cup (225 g) macapuno strings
1 cup (200 g) preserved purple yam
   (ube)
1 (12-oz/340-g) can evaporated milk
Vanilla ice cream, garnish

In 4 tall sundae or milk shake glasses, place ¾ cup (75 g) shaved ice. On top of that, add ¼ cup (approximately 50 g) each of mango, pineapple, jackfruit, macapuno strings, and purple yam. Pour ½ cup (125 ml) evaporated milk and some of the jackfruit juice into each glass. Top the halo-halo with a scoop of vanilla ice cream.

Serve with long ice cream spoons to mix the layers together.

Variation: If you don't feel like buying each ingredient separately, prepared halo-halo fruit mixes are available at the Asian grocer. These convenient, pre-made mixes come in glass jars and, depending on the brand, include a combination of halo-halo staples such as sweetened beans, coconut sport, purple yam, coconut gel, and palm nuts. Place a few spoonfuls of the mix in a glass, then top with shaved ice, evaporated milk, and vanilla ice cream for a nearly instant halo-halo. I find the mixes are a great base to which you can add your favorite fruits such as jackfruit, litchi, banana, mango, papaya, or guava.

TEA CUSTARD EARL GRAY NATILLAS

Overshadowed by the national popularity of *leche flan*, *natilla* may be the obscure Filipino custard, though no lesser in any other comparison. Light and creamy natillas are often called the soft custard, comparable in texture to crème brûlée, which makes it difficult to serve on a fiesta buffet table. Instead, natillas are more suited for individual servings, easily baked in ramekins and dressed with fresh fruit for effortless panache. Earl Gray tea and cream may seem an unlikely pairing for dessert, but the delicate perfume of bergamot oil leaves a sunny citrus essence that charms and calms the palate.

Makes four 4-ounce/125-ml ramekins

1½ cups (375 ml) heavy whipping cream

3 tablespoons granulated sugar

1 Earl Gray tea bag or 1 teaspoon loose tea

3 large egg yolks

½ cup (75 g) ripe strawberries, for garnish (optional)

½ cup (30 g) whipped cream, for garnish (optional)

Preheat the oven to 350°F (175°C). Combine the cream, sugar, and tea in a heavy-bottomed saucepan. Simmer for 5 minutes. Place the egg yolks in a heatproof bowl. While whisking the egg yolks, slowly pour the hot cream into the yolks until all of the cream is incorporated. Strain the mixture through a fine sieve.

Arrange 4 (4-ounce/125-ml) ramekins in a deep baking dish. Ladle the cream mixture into the ramekins and fill the baking dish with water so that it reaches halfway up the sides of the ramekins. Cover the baking dish loosely with aluminum foil and bake for 45 minutes until the centers of the natillas are set but jiggle slightly when tapped.

Remove the baking dish from the oven. Use tongs to remove the ramekins from the water and cool to room temperature. Cover the ramekins with plastic wrap and refrigerate for at least 2 hours before serving.

Garnish with fresh, ripe seasonal strawberries and whipped cream. In the style of crème brûlée, you can caramelize a sugar crust on top of the natillas before serving. Simply sprinkle granulated sugar evenly over the top of the natillas. Use a kitchen blowtorch to caramelize the sugar. If you don't have a blowtorch, place the ramekins underneath the broiler, as close to the flame as possible to caramelize the sugar.

MERINGUE ROLL WITH CHOCOLATE CREAM
CHOCOLATE BRAZO DE MERCEDES

This featherlight cake reminds me of a classic French dessert that's rarely seen on restaurant menus nowadays but still holds timeless quality and absolute satisfaction, *oeufs à la niege*, or poached meringue blanketed with a vanilla sauce of *crème Anglaise*. A traditional *brazo de mercedes* boasts the same alliance of textures and flavors but in the form of a pillowy rolled meringue cake filled with creamy egg custard. Because the cake is very delicate, it requires an airy filling that won't weigh it down. This versatile filling is a simple treasure thickened with egg yolks instead of flour or cornstarch. It starts off pudding-rich but is lightened with whipped cream to make an elegant mousse that can be served alone or spread liberally as a filling or frosting for your cake. To the classic vanilla-flavored *brazo*, I've added cocoa powder and melted, semisweet chocolate morsels for added decadence.

Serves 8

Meringue Cake
8 large egg whites
¾ cup (150 ml) granulated sugar
½ teaspoon cream of tartar

Chocolate Filling
1 (14-oz/420-g) can condensed milk
¼ cup (50 g) semisweet chocolate morsels
1 teaspoon vanilla extract
8 large egg yolks, beaten
1 cup (250 ml) cold heavy whipping cream
2¼ teaspoons unflavored gelatin or 1 gelatin packet

2 tablespoons cocoa powder, for dusting
2 tablespoons confectioners' sugar, for dusting

Make the cake: Preheat the oven to 350°F (175°C). Line a 10 by 15 by 1-inch (25½ by 38 by 2½-cm) jellyroll pan with parchment paper. Place the egg whites in a large mixing bowl. Beat the egg whites with an electric mixer on low speed until frothy. Add the sugar in thirds, beating the whites on high speed to incorporate the sugar.

Once all of the sugar is added, beat the whites to stiff peaks. Pour the batter into the prepared jellyroll pan and evenly smooth the top. Bake for 25 to 30 minutes until the top of the cake has puffed above the rim of the pan and a toothpick inserted into the cake comes out clean. While the cake is baking, prepare the filling.

Make the filling: Combine the condensed milk, chocolate morsels, and vanilla in a heavy-bottom saucepan. Cook the mixture over low-medium heat until the chocolate is completely melted. Whisk the mixture and slowly drizzle the yolks into the pan. Cook the filling slowly over low heat for 5 to 7 minutes, whisking continuously, until a thicklike pudding. Place plastic wrap directly on the surface of the filling (this will prevent a film from forming) and cool to room temperature.

Place the whipped cream in a bowl and whisk to stiff peaks with an electric mixer. Add the gelatin and beat for another 10 seconds to combine. Fold the whipped cream into the cooled chocolate filling and chill in the refrigerator until you are ready to assemble the cake.

Assemble the cake: Remove the cake from the oven and cool for 5 minutes before handling. Combine the cocoa powder and confectioners' sugar in a bowl and stir until well blended. Generously sift the cocoa-sugar mixture evenly over the top of the cake. This will prevent your cake from sticking when unmolded. Invert the cake onto a kitchen towel and peel off the parchment lining, being careful not to tear the meringue. Spread the cooled filling evenly on the bottom of the cake. Starting with a long side, gently roll up the cake and lay the cake seam side down. Chill the cake for 1 hour. Slice into rounds and serve.

Variation: Classic Brazo de Mercedes. This simple meringue cake is paired with a homey vanilla cream filling. It is the basic recipe upon which dozens of variations and flavors of brazo de mercedes are built. Simply omit the cocoa powder and the chocolate morsels from the chocolate recipe. When inverting the cake, use confectioners' sugar instead of cocoa powder.

CASHEW TORTE WITH VANILLA MOUSSE SANS RIVAL

Meaning "without rival," this torte succeeds in earning its name. Three layers of cashew meringue cake are mortared with a light cream that is used as both a filling and frosting. Toasted cashews traditionally decorate the face of the cake, although I've included in this recipe my preference for a chocolate ganache cloak. Admittedly, there are a few steps and components required in assembling a *sans rival*, which might cause you to limit it to special occasions. But the praise you'll receive in addition to future requests for the cake will be worth the effort and perhaps make it a regular indulgence throughout the year.

Serves 6

Filling

¼ cup (50 ml) cold heavy whipping cream
3 tablespoons confectioners' sugar
½ teaspoon vanilla extract
1 packet (2 teaspoons/10 g) unflavored gelatin
¾ cup (175 g) sour cream

Cake

2 cups (275 g) unsalted roasted cashews
1 cup (200 g) granulated sugar
3 tablespoons cornstarch
10 large egg whites
½ cup (50 g) confectioners' sugar, for dusting

Make the filling: Combine the whipping cream, sugar, and vanilla in a mixing bowl. Sprinkle the gelatin over the cream and put the bowl in the refrigerator for 5 minutes; this will keep the cream cold while the gelatin softens. Remove the bowl from the refrigerator and beat the cream with an electric mixer on medium-high speed for 3 minutes until it holds stiff peaks. Add the sour cream and beat another minute to combine. Chill the mixture in the refrigerator until ready to use.

Make the cake: Preheat the oven to 350°F (175°C). Line a 10 by 15-inch (25 by 38-cm) jelly roll pan with parchment paper. Combine the cashews, sugar, and cornstarch in a food processor. Process for 30 seconds until the nuts resemble fine pebbles. Be careful not to overprocess nuts into a paste. Set the ground nuts aside.

Place the egg whites in a large mixing bowl and beat with an electric mixer on low speed until foamy. Gradually add the sugar and increase the speed to high. Beat on high until the egg whites are thick and form stiff peaks. Gently fold the cashew mixture into the egg whites using a rubber spatula. Pour the batter into the prepared jelly roll pan and spread evenly. Bake until golden brown and a toothpick inserted into the center of the cake comes out clean, about 20 minutes. When completely cooled, slide the cake off the jelly roll pan, still attached to the parchment paper.

Assemble the cake: Lay the cake horizontally on your workspace and cut it across its length into thirds, making three equal rectangular pieces. Place one cake layer on a rectangular piece of cardboard cut to fit the cake. Spread one-third of the sour cream filling on the cake. Place the second cake layer on top and spread with more cream. Set the final layer on top. Smooth a thin layer of cream all around the top and sides of the cake and chill for 30 minutes.

Make the chocolate ganache: To make the ganache, combine 8 ounces of semisweet chocolate morsels, 1 tablespoon butter, and ½ cup heavy whipping cream in a microwaveable bowl. Melt on medium-high heat for 2 minutes. Stir the chocolate mixture and cook for another minute until completely melted and smooth. Cool the chocolate for 5 minutes so that it is slightly warm and not hot when poured over the torte.

Position the cake on a cooling rack fitted on a sheet pan or jelly roll pan. Pour the melted chocolate ganache liberally over the top of the torte, smoothing the chocolate over the top and sides of the cake with a flat metal spatula until completely covered. Any drips of chocolate should fall onto the sheet pan. Return the cake to the refrigerator and chill for 30 minutes before serving.

COCONUT-PANDAN TAPIOCA BUKO PANDAN SAGO

Tapioca may seem like an old-fashioned dessert from a bygone era in American history. But like many dishes that fill us with nostalgic comfort, these tender pearls are making a comeback on restaurant menus and in home kitchens alike. Tapioca is made from the gelatinized starch of the cassava plant, a very starchy root native to South America but popularly grown all over the world. This pudding features the beloved *buko pandan* flavor combination that Filipinos are so fond of. Coconut milk steeped with fragrant *pandan* leaves give this wholesome favorite a tropical accent, and slices of caramelized mango on top add a juicy jolt of sweetness. Be sure to use quick-cooking tapioca for speed and ease. Whole or pearl tapioca can be substituted but you'll have to soak it for 10 to 15 minutes (that's for tiny pearls, 30 minutes for large pearls) in warm water to soften it completely before cooking.

Serves 6

1 (13½-oz/400-g) can coconut milk
1½ cups (375 ml) low-fat milk
½ cup (100 g) sugar
1 pandan leaf, approximately 8-in (15-cm) long
1 teaspoon vanilla extract
Dash of salt
½ cup (90 g) quick-cooking tapioca
2 large egg yolks
1 ripe mango (substitute peaches, pineapple, or bananas)
1 tablespoon sugar
½ cup (30 g) whipped cream, for garnish

Make the tapioca: Combine the coconut milk, milk, sugar, pandan leaf, vanilla, and salt in a medium saucepan. Simmer over low heat for 15 minutes to infuse the milk with the pandan. Remove and discard the leaf.

Add the tapioca to the pan and simmer on the lowest heat setting for 5 minutes, stirring frequently to prevent the tapioca from sticking to the bottom of the pan. Add the egg yolks one by one, stirring after each addition and cook for another 5 minutes until the pudding is thick and the tapioca is tender.

Cool the tapioca to room temperature, then chill in the refrigerator for 1 hour before serving.

Caramelize the mango: Position your oven rack directly underneath the broiler. Peel the mango and cut into ½-inch (13-mm) slices. Place the fruit on a greased baking sheet and sprinkle each slice with sugar. Place the mango under a preheated broiler for 1 to 2 minutes until the sugar turns golden brown. Remove from the oven and cool the mango for 5 minutes. Spoon on top of the chilled tapioca with a dollop of whipped cream.

AMBROSIA SHORTCAKE WITH CASSAVA BISCUIT

The classic strawberry shortcake gets a tropical face-lift with this recipe. Grated cassava gives the sweet biscuit a little weight and texture, almost like a scone. Serve the biscuit alone as the perfect teatime snack adorned with little more than butter or whipped cream. Or pair it with a refreshing fruit salad made with summer's bounty of fresh mangoes and strawberries for a lovely finale to dinner, whether it be a fancy affair or a backyard barbecue.

Serves 6

Cassava Biscuit: makes twelve
  2½-in (6½-cm) biscuits
1½ cups (200 g) all-purpose flour
1 cup (225 g) frozen grated cassava,
  thawed and drained
1 tablespoon sugar
1 tablespoon baking powder
¼ teaspoon salt
½ cup (125 g) cold butter, cut into
  thick slices
⅔ cup (150 ml) coconut milk

Fruit Salad
1 mango, peeled, deseeded, and cut
  into ½-in (6-mm) cubes
1 cup (125 g) sliced strawberries
1 (4-oz/125-g) can mandarin
  oranges, drained
1 cup (175 g) fresh pineapple, cut
  into ½-in (6-mm) cubes
¼ cup (50 g) sweetened shredded
  coconut
1 cup (250 ml) whipped cream

Make the biscuit: Preheat the oven to 450°F (230°C). Combine the flour, well-drained cassava, sugar, baking powder, and salt in a food processor. Sprinkle cold butter slices over the flour and pulse the food processor until the mixture resembles coarse crumbs. Pour in the coconut milk and pulse until the dough barely just comes together.

Turn the mixture onto a well-floured surface and flatten to a 1-inch (2½-cm) thickness. Use 2½-inch (6½-cm)-round biscuit cutters to cut 12 biscuits. Place the biscuits on a baking sheet. Lightly brush the tops of the biscuits with melted butter and sprinkle with sugar. Bake for 12 to 15 minutes until golden brown. Cool on a wire rack for 5 minutes. Use a serrated knife to split the biscuits in half horizontally.

Make the salad and assemble the shortcakes: Combine the mango, strawberries, mandarin oranges, pineapple, and coconut in a large bowl. Toss together. Place the bottom of the biscuit on a plate. Spoon the fruit salad onto the biscuit. Top with whipped cream (or vanilla ice cream) and lay the top of the biscuit over the cream. Serve immediately with extra whipped cream.

BANANA, CHOCOLATE, AND COCONUT EGG ROLLS TURON

These egg rolls were not so much dessert in my house as they were *merienda* fare, a light midmorning or midafternoon snack served with coffee or hot chocolate. The banana-chocolate-coconut combination is a personal favorite of mine, although not one that I grew up with. (Macapuno strings, a variety of the coconut palm plant, also called coconut sport, adds a signature Filipino flavor and pleasingly chewy texture.) The classic *turon* of my youth was filled with slices of ripe plantain and juicy jackfruit for a warm crispy snack that was just sweet enough to be considered a treat. These rolls are literally a cinch to make and a treasure to have stashed in the freezer as an impressive offering for the unexpected guest or merely as an indulgence to satisfy your own sweet tooth.

Makes 12 turon

1 package (25 sheets) lumpia wrappers or super-thin spring roll wrappers, defrosted
3 bananas, peeled
1 cup (200 g) semisweet chocolate morsels
1 (12-oz/340-g) jar macapuno strings
1 large egg, beaten
2 to 3 cups (500 to 750 ml) oil, for frying

Prepare the wrappers and bananas: Gently pull the wrappers apart, being careful not to tear them. Once separated, cover the wrappers with plastic wrap or a towel to keep them from drying out until you are ready to use them.

Slice the bananas in half lengthwise, then again across the center so that there are 4 halves per banana, 12 pieces in total.

Assemble the egg rolls: Position a wrapper on your workspace so that the square faces you. Center a banana, cut side down, ½ inch (13 mm) above the bottom edge of the wrapper. Spoon about a tablespoon of macapuno strings on the banana, then sprinkle a few chocolate morsels on top of the macapuno. Use your fingers to lift the bottom edge over the filling. Roll the banana once tightly then fold in both sides toward the center. Brush the top edge with the egg. Roll up the egg roll and press to seal. Take another wrapper, this time with a corner facing you. Wrap your egg roll a second time using the same method. This will ensure that the filling will not leak out into the oil and burn.

Place the filled egg rolls on a platter, seal-side down, covered with a towel to keep from drying out. Repeat with the remaining bananas.

Cook the egg rolls: Heat the oil in a frying pan to 350°F (175°C). Cook the egg rolls 3 to 5 minutes, turning them so that they brown evenly on all sides. Remove from the oil and drain on paper towels. Serve immediately.

Variation: Cinnamon-spiced apples and canned jackfruit make an excellent combination in turon. In a large skillet combine 2½ pounds (1¼ kg) apples, peeled, cored, and sliced; 2 tablespoons butter; ½ cup (115 g) brown sugar, 1 teaspoon ground cinnamon, and ¼ teaspoon ground ginger. Cook and stir over medium heat until the apples are tender, about 15 minutes. Cool the apple mixture. Drain and slice the jackfruit into thin strips.

BUYING FILIPINO INGREDIENTS

Many cooks already know that a meal does not begin in the kitchen but at the market. The beauty of Filipino cookery is that a good number of the spices, condiments, and ingredients needed for these recipes are readily available in your neighborhood grocery store, if they aren't already in your cupboard or refrigerator. Many large grocery store chains have updated their ethnic foods section to include a wide variety of Asian and Latino ingredients used in these recipes. However, if you happen to be lucky enough to have an Asian grocery store available to you, take advantage of it.

This chapter will help you shed your fear of the unknown bottles, jars, and bags that are indispensable to the Asian cook. Although I am not entirely against ingredient substitutions, I will say that they will take a recipe so far and should be used conscientiously. Once you've become familiar with the ingredients and how they affect the recipe, choosing substitutions will become easier. If you stick to substituting similar flavors, you usually won't go astray. For example, it's safe to substitute sambal ulek for Thai chiles or lime for calamansi or fish sauce for shrimp paste. However, swapping soy sauce for fish sauce will not give you the results you want when they both lend such different flavors to a dish. Using the proper ingredients will be the difference between a good recipe and an amazing meal.

This shopping guide is organized very similarly to an Asian market. When you walk in an Asian market you'll often start off with large sacks of rice towering high in the first corner aisle. Weighing at least as much as a small child, these bags hold rice in dozens of varieties, colors, shapes, and sizes, which is why I start this chapter with a few of the main selections you're likely to encounter. Then, as you meander through the store, you'll find aisles dedicated to the mind-boggling selection of noodles and condiments, dried herbs, spices, and canned goods before arriving at the refrigerated area where the exotic spread of produce is displayed alongside all of the frozen foods. Though it may seem odd, I've inserted a special section on coconut. The coconut plant is a thriving Filipino resource, so much so that coconut products represent an important component of the cuisine.

You won't necessarily have to search out a Filipino market to find these ingredients. I often find everything I need for a Filipino meal at a Thai, Vietnamese, or Chinese market. And if Asian markets are scarce in your area, the Mail-Order and Online Shopping Guide (page 175) will prove helpful in securing those hard-to-find ingredients.

Rice is the single most important element of Filipino cuisine, the reason to eat. Often, main courses and side dishes take a back seat to rice, serving merely as toppings or condiments. There are thousands of rice varieties classified by their grain length: short, medium, or long. Short and medium grains cook moist and tender with a slight stickiness. Long grains cook separate and fluffy. Carolina rice, basmati, and brown rice are all in the long-grain category. Most Asian stores will carry enough rice varieties for the average shopper to be slightly intimidated by the mountains of paper and burlap rice bags. The following are the types of rice you should look for when shopping for a Filipino meal. Rely on your personal preference when choosing between long- and medium-grain rice for your everyday rice. Short-grain and glutinous rice are not commonly used as all-purpose table rice but for specific dishes.

Long-Grain Rice. Long-grain, or indica, varieties, are the most commonly grown rice in the Philippines. Having little starch, long-grain rice cooks to a tender, separate, and fluffy texture with just enough fresh-cooked stickiness to satisfy the Filipino palate. Jasmine rice, originally grown in Thailand but now available from California, is a naturally aromatic long-grain variety that cooks tender and sticky like a medium-grain rice, which is why it is a popular rice among Filipinos. Because the grains easily separate, long-grain rice is great for pilafs or curries. Filipinos love the dry, day-old texture of long-grain rice for *sinangag*, a breakfast staple of garlic fried rice.

Medium-Grain Rice. This is another all-purpose table rice. The grains are shorter and wider than long-grain rice and cook up soft, plump, and sticky. The medium-grain *japonica* rice variety, also called calrose rice, is quite a multitasker making frequent appearances in porridge, stuffings, and soups. Popular brands are Botan Extra Fancy Calrose, Nishiki Premium, and Ichiban Premium.

Short-Grain Rice. Short-grain rice, also called sushi rice, has nearly round, plump kernels that cook into clumps of soft, sticky grains. Short-grain rice is most commonly used for sushi, puddings, and molded rice dishes. Brands to look for are Kukoho Rose, Assi, Yume Super Premium, Nozomi Super Premium, or Nishimoto.

Glutinous Rice. This type of rice is also known as sticky rice, sweet rice, or mochi rice. The name of this rice is deceiving in that it does not have any noticeable sugar sweetness in flavor nor does it have gluten. When raw, the short, round orbs are an opaque, chalky white that when cooked become translucent and extremely sticky. Glutinous rice is not an everyday rice but specific to desserts, puddings, and wrapped or steamed snacks.

Rice Flour and Glutinous Rice Flour. Made from milled long-grain rice, rice flour is used commercially to make noodles and egg roll or dumpling wrappers and noncommercially for dumplings, cakes, and other desserts. Glutinous rice flour is made from milled short-grain glutinous rice and is used to make doughs, heavy batters, and desserts with a heavier texture. Not often is rice flour used as a thickening agent as are wheat flour or cornstarch.

Black Rice. Black rice, called *pirurutong*, has only recently come into the limelight on restaurant menus and grocery store shelves, but it's been a longtime standard in Asia. When purchasing black rice, you will find either Thai black sticky rice or Chinese forbidden black rice. The Thai variety is a medium-grain rice and is often referred to as black glutinous rice, although it lacks the characteristic stickiness of white, short-grained glutinous rice. Closely resembling wild rice, Thai black rice is a whole grain that gets its uneven purple-black color from the exposed outer bran, which also imparts a woody flavor to the rice.

Chinese black rice, or "forbidden" rice, is another medium-grain rice, although not of the glutinous variety. For a time it was served exclusively to Chinese emperors, but now this nearly extinct rice variety has gained popularity on tables around the world as a nutritious, whole-grain substitute to polished white rice.

Interestingly, the black rice varieties are not terribly popular in their mother countries except in sweet snacks or dessert puddings. Steamed white rice will always reign supreme on the Asian table as the everyday rice. But for Western palates, the nutty chewy texture of black rice is welcomed in savory side dishes and salads. I use black rice in Paella Pirurutong a la Filipina (page 76).

The Chinese culinary influence extends far beyond the common Filipino use of soy sauce or ginger to include the fundamental noodle dishes that are collectively called *pancit*. Although a general term, pancit is considered a national dish because most regions throughout the many islands have some form of it. The different kinds of pancit are often distinguished in name by the type of noodle used or by the region in which it is popular.

Dried Rice Vermicelli, Thin Rice Stick Noodles (*Bihon*). These dried noodles are thin round threads made from rice flour and water. They can be added directly to simmering liquid to cook, but I find that softening the noodles in warm water beforehand makes them easier to use. Pancit Palabok is made with *bihon* noodles.

Chinese Wheat Noodles (*Pancit Miki*). Also known as Shanghai-style noodles, these noodles are made solely with wheat flour and water and available fresh in small plastic packages that look very similar to flat fettuccine or round spaghetti. Miki noodles are also available dried in boxes in varying shapes (round or flat) and thickness. Any yellow color that they may have is artificial.

Chinese Egg Noodles (*Pancit Mami*). The egg in mami noodles lends a rich chewy texture to this type of pancit. They are similar in appearance to the fresh Chinese wheat noodles described above, except that their coloring may be slightly more yellow (again, due to artificial coloring). Mami noodles are available in two shapes: thick and round, or thin and flat like fettuccine, and it is most commonly used in noodle soups.

Super-Fine Wheat Noodle Sticks (*Misua*). These dried noodles are thread-thin and cook almost instantly. They have a silky smooth texture, not at all like other noodles and must be added at the very last moments of cooking.

Mung Bean Thread Noodles (*Sotanghon*). Also called bean thread vermicelli, these dried sotanghon noodles are made from mung bean flour and water. They require soaking in warm water to soften them before cooking. Once softened, they have a slick, jellylike translucent appearance. These noodles are easy to distinguish in the grocery store since they are often packaged in neon pink netting.

Thick Chinese-Style Instant Noodles (*Pancit Canton, Pancit Mian, Pancit Lomi*). Canton noodles are dried instant wheat noodles often made with coconut oil and yellow food coloring. The noodles cook very quickly and are added to the pancit broth toward the end of the cooking process.

Cornstarch Noodles (*Pancit Luglug*). These dried noodles are long round strands that must be soaked in warm to hot water to soften before using. They appear creamy and opaque white when dried, and translucent when soaked or cooked.

Banana Leaves. *See page 167.*

Egg Roll and Dumpling Wrappers.
Lumpia is a generic Filipino term for egg roll. Since there are many types of egg rolls, there follow many different types of lumpia wrappers. You will find most of these wrappers in the frozen or refrigerated section in many sizes, shapes, and colors. The following are the more popular types of wrappers used for the recipes in this book:

Egg Roll Wrappers. These thin dough sheets are made with wheat flour, egg, and water. They come in 7 to 8-inch (17½ to 20-cm) square sheets in packages of twenty-five (11 ounces). When fried, the wrappers turn a crispy golden brown with small bubbles rippling the surface of the wrappers.

Lumpia Wrappers. Specifically labeled *lumpia* wrappers are translucent, superthin round skins made from cornstarch or flour, egg, and water (shown to the right). They are similar to the spring roll wrappers in the way they cook, light and crispy. They are offered in 8-inch (20-cm) square blocks or 10-inch (25-cm) rounds. You'll find both sizes in the frozen section of your Asian market. Make sure the wrappers are completely thawed before using. Once thawed, you will have to separate the wrappers by gently peeling each sheet from the stack. Lumpia wrappers dry out quickly and become difficult to use so keep them covered with a towel or in a freezer bag until you're ready to use them.

Spring Roll Wrappers. These Chinese-style, ultrathin square wrappers look similar to the thicker egg roll wrappers but are made without egg and have a more transparent look to them. When fried to a golden brown, the surface of the wrapper remains smooth and crispy, like a crunchy thin wafer. Spring roll wrappers are usually found frozen in a stack of twenty-five sheets. Treat spring roll wrappers as you would frozen lumpia wrappers, allowing them to thaw before separating the thin sheets.

Vietnamese Rice Paper Wrappers.
These dried wrappers are not typically used in Filipino cuisine but instead are an excellent substitute when spring roll wrappers or lumpia wrappers are unavailable. Made with rice flour and water, these dried round sheets come in different sizes, most commonly 12, 10, and 6½ inches (30, 25, and 16 cm) in diameter. I prefer using the 6½ inch (16 cm), which doesn't require cutting into smaller pieces, as do the larger sizes. Because they are dried, they require softening before being filled and fried. Fill a large pie dish with hot tap water. Dip each wrapper into the water for 30 seconds to 1 minute until the wrappers are soft and pliable. Remove from the water and place on your work surface. The wrappers are then ready to fill and roll; they can be used for fresh spring rolls or deep-fried to make egg rolls. You'll find the wrappers in the dried noodles aisle; they're easy to pick out with their beautiful crosshatch imprint resulting from the bamboo mats on which the wrappers are dried.

COCONUT

In the Philippines coconuts are an essential economic and household commodity with its valuable flesh prized as a source of coconut milk and other edible coconut products. However, Filipinos use the entire coconut to their advantage: the shells are made into utensils and musical instruments; the fronds can be woven into mats, hats, baskets, and brooms or layered for thatching material; and the copra (white coconut flesh) yields coconut oil used for cooking, making soaps, shampoos, perfumes, and cosmetics.

The recipes in this book will refer to coconut juice (also called coconut water), coconut milk, and coconut cream. With the exception of the Chaokoh brand of coconut milk (useful when making coconut cream), I don't seek a particular brand of coconut juice, milk, or cream because there are so many available from India, Thailand, Vietnam, and the Philippines with relative homogeneity among them. These are their relative definitions:

Coconut Juice/Coconut Water. This is the clear liquid found in the center of a fresh coconut. It is not often used for cooking but enjoyed freshly poured from the coconut as a beverage. In Asian countries or even Asian neighborhoods in the United States, it is quite common to see tourists and locals sipping coconut juice from long straws inserted into a hole poked into the top of a coconut.

Coconut Milk. This is made from the toughened white meat of mature brown coconuts. The meat is grated and moistened with water, gathered in cheesecloth, and pressed. The first press yields thick coconut cream. More water is added to the coconut meat for a second press, which produces thick coconut milk. A third press produces thin coconut milk.

Coconut Cream. Coconut cream is essentially a thick pastelike version of coconut milk, it is the first press of coconut and water. You can find coconut cream in the frozen section or you can easily make it yourself using canned coconut milk. Depending on the brand of coconut milk, I have found that coconut cream may be obtained in one of two ways. The first is by far the simplest: chilling a can of coconut milk in the refrigerator and allowing the coconut solids to separate from the water. Remember, coconut milk is just grated coconut and water. The coconut solids will often form a firm mass at the top of the can, which is easily separated from the water by pouring the contents through cheesecloth or a fine sieve. The water, which appears cloudy white, can be saved and used as a cooking liquid for soups, stews, or stir-fries. The strained solids or coconut cream is what you have left to use in your recipe. The Chaokoh brand of coconut milk is excellent and has an impressive amount of coconut cream that easily separates from its liquid when using the chilling method. The second method, for which any brand of coconut milk works equally well, requires reducing the water out of the coconut milk by cooking it over low heat, whisking occasionally to keep the oils from separating from the solids. See page 16 for instructions on making cooked coconut cream.

Other Coconut Products

Macapuno. This is a mutant variety of the coconut palm plant that produces large coconuts that do not have the characteristic water in the center of the fruit. Macapuno tastes like coconut but has a soft jellylike texture compared to the firm dry flesh of a mature coconut. Also called coconut sport, macapuno comes in long strands, preserved in sugar, and packed in glass jars. It is commonly used in desserts for custards, *halo-halo* (Filipino sundae), cakes, or pies.

Nata de Coco. The Philippines is the birthplace of this unique product. Also labeled coconut gel, *nata de coco* is a firm, chewy, translucent jellylike dessert made when bacteria is added to coconut water found in the center of the coconut fruit and allowed to ferment for several weeks. Nata de coco comes either canned or jarred in sugared syrup and is eaten plain or added to beverages and desserts. It is a common addition to *halo-halo*, a shaved ice dessert of layered fruit and sweetmeats.

Buko. Buko refers to tender, young coconut meat from an immature coconut. Most of what Americans see and use in the way of coconut is the meat from mature brown coconuts, which is firm and relatively dry. Young coconut meat is moist and tender with a consistency of a very ripe pear.

Coconut Vinegar. *See page 174.*

Annatto Seeds (*Atsuete*). Native to South America, these pebble-sized, rust-colored seeds came to the Philippines via the Spanish. Annatto seeds have almost no odor and a faint dusty flavor but are prized for their bright russet color. Filipinos sauté annatto seeds with olive oil to impart the characteristic flavor and vibrant color to a dish.

Bagoong. Bagoong refers to the generous category of fermented seafood sauces and pastes. Bagoong uses different types of seafood, ranging from oysters to clams to fish to shrimp. **Bagoong Alamang**, also called *guinamos*, is often labeled shrimp fry or shrimp paste. It is a bright purple-pink or pink-gray paste made from fermented shrimp. It is very salty and is used to enhance the flavor of soups, sauces, meats, or fish. Bagoong alamang is commonly used as a condiment sautéed with garlic, tomatoes, onions, or chiles (called *bagoong guisado*) and is served on the table as a finishing flavor paste. **Bagoong Balayan**, like bagoong monamon, is made from fermented anchovies and round scad but it is a thin liquid sauce instead of a paste. **Bagoong Monamon** is a gray paste made from fermented anchovies and round scad.

Banana Ketchup/Banana Sauce. This is as popular a condiment in the Philippines as tomato ketchup is in the States. Although the primary ingredient is banana, you'd never know it by the look or taste. Both the ketchup and sauce are artificially colored red and were it not for the distinctive sweet and spicy finish, one could easily mistake it for tomato ketchup. It's used as a basting sauce or dipping sauce for barbecued chicken or meats and, of course, on hamburgers and French fries. You'll find bottled banana ketchup in the condiments section of the Asian market.

Banana Leaves. These are the large green leathery leaves of the banana tree. They are most commonly available in plastic packages of frozen whole leaves, stacked one upon another and folded into large rectangles. Banana leaves are a popular wrapper for steamed or grilled dishes because of the light flavor that they impart as well as the protection they provide the meats or fish over direct heat.

Banana Varieties. Filipinos hold the banana in high regard and are not limited by the fruit when it comes to creative uses. As the largest fruit industry on the islands, bananas are serious business in the Philippines. Saba cooking bananas are the most widely grown, followed by the variety most commonly eaten in the States, Cavendish bananas. Saba bananas are primarily used in the Philippines as a cooking banana when green or semi-ripe. However, when they fully ripen, as indicated by their dark yellow skin, they are deliciously sweet eaten uncooked. Plantains are a fine, although not exact, substitute for Sabas.

Bok Choi. Also referred to as Shanghai bok choi, pak-choi, or baby bok choi, this member of the cabbage family has a pale green base and stalk from which tender green leaves shoot out. Bok choi is very popular in Filipino cooking as a substitute for Napa cabbage because its small size allows cooks to cook the whole thing quickly, without slicing or shredding.

Calamansi or Kalamansi. Regional dialects allow for both spellings of this fruit. Native to the Philippines, this small gum ball–sized citrus fruit is delicious and versatile with a flavor that lies somewhere in the intersection of a lemon, lime, and mandarin orange. It's that good. The pale yellow–orange flesh is very tart and used as a finishing condiment squeezed over noodles or grilled foods. It is also juiced, diluted with water, and sweetened with sugar to make a delicious beverage. Served hot, it makes a soothing tea; served cold, it is a refreshing thirst quencher. Fresh calamansi will be sold in netted bags and keep for about 1 week. Alternatives to fresh calamansi are frozen packets of pure calamansi juice and bottled, presweetened calamansi concentrate.

Cassava (*Kamote Kahoy*). Native to South America, cassava (also known as yucca or manioc) is a long dark brown, starchy root with a tough, sometimes waxy exterior peel and firm, ivory white flesh. Most Americans are familiar with cassava in its processed form of tapioca pearls, which are made from gelatinized cassava starch. Cooks in Hispanic and Southeast Asian countries embrace cassava's versatility using it in its fresh form as you would use a potato: sliced into chunks for stews, simmered and mashed as a side dish, or grated and mixed into a batter for steamed savory snacks. In Filipino cuisine, cassava is primarily used for baking because of its heavy starch content, which makes it an ideal substitute for wheat flour.

In the grocery store, you may find the 1 to 2-foot (30½ to 61-cm)-long, dark brown tubers fresh in the vegetable section. Choose cassava that are hard and dense and have dark brown unblemished skin. The size of cassava, which can range in length from only a few inches to nearly 2 feet (30 cm), is not particularly important when choosing fresh cassava. When preparing fresh cassava, first peel off the brown skin with a peeler or a paring knife to reveal

the white flesh. Any black striations in the flesh indicate that the cassava is getting old although it is still edible when cooked. If you don't plan on using your cassava right away, store it in a cool dry place for up to 4 days.

If cassava is not available fresh, you may buy the frozen versions that come in different forms: peeled, whole cassava cut into 2 to 3-inch (5 to 7½-cm) pieces, or finely grated in 14 to 16-ounce (400 to 450-g) packages.

Chayote (*Sayote*). A Mexican native, chayote is another Spanish import that belongs to the extended squash family. Like its summer squash relatives, chayote can be eaten either raw or cooked. The flavor is rather weak but it has a firm body, which makes it very versatile in almost any type of preparation from soups to stews to pickles. In the Filipino kitchen, chayote makes an equitable substitute for green papaya in cooked dishes.

Chinese Celery (*Kinchay*). Chinese celery is easily distinguishable from the more common European celery

that Americans are familiar with. The thin almost spindly stalks are crisp and less fibrous and are topped by plentiful bushy leaves that slightly resemble flat-leaf parsley. The flavor of Chinese celery is more assertive than regular celery and it is an important vegetable in stir-fries and soups.

Chinese Long Beans (*Sitao*). Also called yard-long beans, Chinese long beans look and taste deceivingly like a member of the green bean family when, in fact, they are cousins to black-eyed peas. Growing up to 3 feet (90 cm) in length, long beans are easy to find in almost every Asian grocery store coiled in looped bundles or rubber-banded into roped bunches. You'll find one of two common varieties on the shelves: the first is pale green with a full firm body; the second variety is dark green and pencil-thin. When purchasing, look for beans that are free of dark spots or blemishes and that have a good bright color. They are best 1 to 1½-feet (30 to 45-cm) long, which is when they are at their tender peak. Longer beans are older and become tough with age. Even though long beans are pliable, they should not be withered or limp. Cook them as you would green beans.

Chinese Red Dates. Also called Chinese jujube or zizyphi fructose, these Chinese dates come dried with or without their seeds. Often used as a medicinal fruit in Chinese culture to remedy the heart, lungs, and stomach, these dates are oblong in shape and dark reddish brown in color and have a sweet-tart flavor.

Chinese Sausage. These thin cured sausages (shown in the top left side of the photograph below) are made from pork, beef, or both with salt, sugar, honey, and spices. The sausages are vacuum packaged in the refrigerated section and have a distinct sweet and savory flavor. They may be sliced like salami and added to vegetable or noodle dishes or simply fried or steamed and served with rice.

Chorizo De Bilbao. Not in any way related to or originating from Bilbao, Spain, chorizo de Bilbao (shown in the lower right-hand side of the photograph above) is a generic Filipino term for any version of a Spanish-style, semi-cured sausage. It is heavily flavored with paprika and garlic and used widely in different stuffings and noodle dishes.

Daikon Radish (Labanos). This root vegetable is much larger than the small red radishes we are used to seeing. It has a smooth white surface and grows to 2 to 4 inches in diameter and 6 inches to 2 feet long. Daikon radishes are mild in piquancy and are a versatile vegetable served raw in salads or cooked in soups or stews.

Dried Anchovies (Dilis). Eaten fresh, canned, dried, or processed into precious *bagoong* fish paste, the local anchovy industry is an important component of Filipino cuisine. Dried anchovies come in varying sizes from very tiny to finger-length and are a popular snack, fried and dipped into spicy vinegar or soy sauce.

Dried Mushrooms. In many Asian grocery stores there are almost as many types of dried mushrooms as there are dried noodles. They are often called Chinese mushrooms or dried shiitake mushrooms and have brown caps with beige shriveled stems. They range in variety and price depending on the type, size, and quality of the mushroom. Dried mushrooms must be soaked for 15 to 30 minutes until they are soft and plump and easy to slice. The soaking liquid is concentrated mushroom flavor that begs to be used in soups or broths. Do strain the liquid through a fine sieve; the mushrooms often leave behind dirt and debris after soaking.

Dried Shrimp. Dried shrimp is a common ingredient in Asian cuisine used not only to season seafood dishes but meats, poultry, and vegetables. Like fish sauce or oyster sauce, dried shrimp has the undeniable odor of the sea but when cooked imparts a full dimensional flavor that is not overpowering fishy. These tiny shrimp come in many forms

and sizes. Large shrimp (roughly ½ inch/1 cm in length) often come peeled without the head. The extra small shrimp (¼ inch/6 mm long) are featherlight and dried with the shells and heads left on.

Fermented Black Beans. Salted black soybeans are fermented with spices to produce a pungent flavor that lends a dish earthy taste and rich texture. It is often recommended to rinse these beans before cooking to remove some of the salt and to lessen the intensity of their flavor. But I find that rinsing defeats the purpose of having the precious beans in the dish at all. Fermented black beans are often used in braising meats or steaming fish or poultry.

Fish Sauce (Patis). Fish sauce is Southeast Asia's equivalent to soy sauce. As a general rule, when I cook any type of Asian dish, I use fish sauce for seafood dishes and soy sauce for meat and poultry. It is a thin, light-colored liquid made from fermented anchovies or other small fish. The extract is very salty and has a formidable fishy odor that easily discourages the unaware cook. However, the flavor that fish sauce lends to your food is not the same one that assaults you upon opening the bottle, but one of subtle harmony and balance. Fish sauce can be used as a dipping sauce mixed with lime, chiles, or garlic, or as a seasoning for foods during cooking.

Ginger (*Luya*). This flavorsome rhizome is essential to many Asian cuisines, including Filipino. The thick knobby fingers are covered with a thin beige skin that covers the juicy pale yellow flesh. Look for gingerroot whose skin is smooth and unblemished indicating tender, young flavorful flesh. Once peeled, ginger may be minced, sliced, grated, or even used in large chunks to lend its piquant flavor and aroma to soups, stews, or stir-fries.

Green Mango. Green mangoes are simply mangoes picked before they have ripened into the sweet juicy fruit enjoyed worldwide. In this immature form, green mangoes are eaten as a tart snack dipped in fish sauce or shrimp paste. Green mangoes are very sour and have pale green to yellow flesh. When choosing green mangos look for green skin with no yellow or red colorations that indicate ripening. The fruit should be very hard and should not have any distinct mango smell. Green mangoes are sold at Asian markets.

Green Papaya. This is merely green or unripe papaya. Green papaya is rich in the enzyme papain, a natural digestive aid, which diminishes as the papaya ripens and is nonexistent in fully ripe papaya. The tropical fruit has dark green skin with white to pale green flesh and a loose cluster of white seeds in the center. Once peeled, the flavor of green papaya is not sweet but faintly

grassy. The firm flesh, which has a crisp crunchy texture, is served raw in salads and pickles, or cooked in soups, stews, or stir-fries. As a general rule, cook green papaya the same way you would zucchini. A comparable substitute for cooked green papaya is the chayote; however, it is not a suitable substitute for recipes that call for raw green papaya.

Hoisin Sauce. Hoisin is the Asian equivalent to an American barbecue sauce. It is a heavy, dark brown paste made from salted soybeans, sugar, vinegar, and spices. Hoisin is often used as a glaze or marinade for grilled meats and poultry or as a tangy dipping sauce for egg rolls and spring rolls.

Horseradish Leaves (*Malunggay*). The horseradish tree is native to India and has long branches of small, oval-shaped concentrated leaflets that make an excellent alternative to spinach. Young horseradish leaves have a mild peppery flavor and are highly nutritious as an excellent source of vitamins A, C, and B, iron, and calcium. Only sporadically have I had the pleasure of

finding fresh horseradish leaves at the Asian grocer. You'll find them on long thin branches rubber-banded together, perhaps loosely wrapped in cellophane. Grab them when you do find them since they make a beautiful addition to your salads, soups, and sautés

Jackfruit (*Nangka* or *Langka*). Jackfruit is a large intimidating-looking fruit that is not commonly found fresh in the Asian grocery store. You'll more likely find it frozen, the yellow fruit pods tidily shrink-wrapped in packages or large sections of the whole fruit cut into 3 to 4-pound (1¼ to 1¾-kg) segments.

Jackfruit is the largest tree fruit in the world (just think of a watermelon hanging from a tree), weighing as much as 80 pounds (36-¼ kg). It has a strongly scented, heavily studded armor shell that oozes a sticky sap once cut. Inside, the fruit is a series of yellow pods which when ripe are sweet and juicy. This yellow fruit covers a large seed that is also edible when cooked. Jackfruit is more commonly and conveniently available in the canned fruit section packed in sweetened juice. I love using jackfruit in both sweet and savory dishes as an alternative to sugar because of the unique sweetness that gives depth to many dishes.

Jicama (*Sinkamas*). This tuber is also called the yam bean, Mexican potato, or Chinese turnip. It is round with thin, tan skin and milky white flesh underneath. Jicama has a mild unassuming flavor and is valued primarily for its apple-crisp crunchy texture. It is wonderful served raw in salads because it takes on the flavor of any dressing. However, it also makes a cheap suitable substitute for water chestnuts in Asian stir-fries for added texture. Choose jicama with thin, smooth unblemished skin that indicates young nonfibrous flesh underneath.

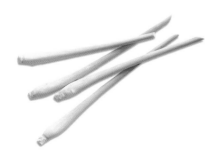

Lemongrass (*Tanglad*). Lemongrass is an oddly shaped herb with its small bulbous base that connects to the long pale yellow stalk. The usable base and heart lend a distinct lemon essence without any acidity. Remove the tough outer layers of the stalk and cut above the tender pinkish bulb, which you should bruise slightly with the flat side of your knife to release the lemon perfume. If minced finely, lemongrass is edible. But if cut into large rings or chunks, discard the pieces as you would a bay leaf or whole peppercorn.

Lycium. Lycium's magical healing powers have been the subject of Chinese folklore, poetry, and celebrations, and not entirely without cause. It has more beta carotene than carrots, which is why the Chinese use it as a cure for failing eyesight. It also claims similar benefits recognized in the berry family (raspberries, cranberries) such as high levels of vitamin C and E, two powerful antioxidants that boost the body's immune system. This small, raisin-sized berry is used by Chinese herbalists to improve circulation, protect the liver and kidneys, reduce fever, and control high blood pressure. I enjoy using lycium because the bright red berries add a splash of color to any dish, but also because of its wonderful sweet-tart flavor. These berries are usually found in the tea or herbal aisle of your Asian grocery store nestled somewhere in between ginseng and lotus seeds. They are dried and packaged in individual bags or prepackaged with other dried herbs. I add the dried berries to soups or stews so that they absorb the cooking liquid to become plump red orbs. It is also known as the Chinese wolfberry.

Mirin. Mirin is not a Filipino staple but one that I enjoy adding to Filipino dishes. Popular in Japanese cuisine, mirin is a sweet rice wine made from fermented glutinous rice. It has a very high sugar content that easily masks its alcohol flavor. The Japanese use mirin mainly for cooking, but I find it an invaluable addition to salad dressings, sauces, and meat marinades.

Misu. Called miso, this thick rust-colored paste resembles peanut butter in its color, thickness, and high protein content. Made from fermented soybeans, yeast, and malted grain, this paste is used to flavor soups, sauces, dressings, and marinades.

Mung Beans (*Mongo*). Mung beans are native to India but eaten throughout China and Southeast Asia. These small round beans are dark green when whole and bright yellow when stripped of their outer layer. Mung beans are easy to cook and don't require presoaking like other dried beans. Yellow mung beans cook in half the time it takes for green mung beans to cook, and when well-cooked have a wonderful creamy consistency. Mung beans are a common ingredient ground into flour to make cellophane noodles, mashed into a sweetened paste for cakes and snacks, and as a nutritious protein alternative in soups and stews.

Napa Cabbage (*Pechay*). Chinese Pe-tsai or pechay in Filipino is the oblong tender cabbage with wide white ribs and pale green leaves. It has tender leaves that have a sweet flavor when eaten raw in salads, pickled, or wilted in soups. This is my preferred cabbage for Filipino recipes because of its tenderness, sweetness, and its short cooking time.

Oyster Sauce. Running a close second to soy sauce in Asian cooking is oyster sauce. This brown creamy sauce is made from a steamed mixture of oysters, sugar, salt, wheat flour, cornstarch, and caramel. Oyster sauce has a rich earthy flavor not indicative of the oyster extracts and is versatile as a harmonious addition to vegetables, meats, poultry, seafood, and noodles.

Pandan, Screw Pine Leaf. The long, thin fragrant leaves are from the screw pine tree. Pandan leaves impart a tropical green flavor and are used to scent any number of dishes from steamed rice to desserts. The versatile leaves are used as wrapping for rice snacks or grilled meats, seafood, or poultry. I've also seen them formed into a basting brush used to impart its aroma on grilled meats, poultry, or fish. Pandan may also be ground to a pulp and used as an extract to lend its deep green color and flavor to cakes, pastries, and other desserts. Pandan leaves come in different

forms. If you're lucky, you'll find them fresh in the produce section of the Asian market. Otherwise, they're available canned, frozen, or in extract form.

Pili Nuts. These nuts grow throughout the Pacific Islands, Southeast Asia, and Australia, although the Philippines claims to be the only commercial producer. Pili nuts boast the highest oil content of all nuts, rivaling macadamia nuts in this category with over 70 percent fat. But what all this fat lends to the pili nut is a creamy richness that makes it delicious and indulgent. I have had difficulty finding pili nuts in the United States other than in candied form with a thin, hard caramel coating, which is how I've used it in this recipe collection. They are also called java almond, kenari nut, Philippine nut.

Plantains. These thick oversized bananas are strictly cooking bananas. Because of their high starch content, they are eaten as a vegetable instead of a fruit. Although Filipinos primarily use the Saba banana variety, plantains are an excellent substitute and readily available in mainstream and Latino grocery stores. When unripe, the thick

skin will be green and the plantain will be very hard and starchy. As it ripens, the skin turns golden yellow with black striations and the fruit turns sweet while remaining firm. Eventually at full ripeness, the skin turns black and the inside fruit becomes tender. Plantains can be eaten at each stage of maturity.

Pork Crackling (*Chicharon*). Crispy pork skin (rind) is commonly eaten as a Filipino snack or used as a meaty addition to vegetable and noodle dishes. Although pork is the *chicharon* of choice, Filipinos also include crispy fried fish skin or chicken skin in this category. Pork chicharon is easily made by trimming the thick layer of fat and skin from roast cuts of pork belly or shoulder. The skin is cut into chunks and either fried or roasted until crispy. Good-quality chicharon is easily found in Latino markets.

Rice Wine (*Tapuy*). Rice wine is a traditional drink made regionally in the northern provinces of Luzon. It is a small localized industry, which doesn't have widespread, commercial availability. However, Chinese rice wine is commonly available and is an excellent substitute.

Sambal Ulek. The Indonesian word *sambal* is a general name for any spicy chili sauce for raw or cooked foods. There are many different types of sambal, ranging from fiery hot to mild to sweet. *Ulek* refers to the mortar and specially-shaped pestle, the *ulek-ulek*, used to grind the chiles into a paste. Often, different commercial brands of *sambal ulek* will include vinegar, garlic, or sugar, which add extra flavor to dishes beyond fiery heat. But I prefer purchasing a clean sambal ulek made with just chiles and perhaps salt, which allows me to add heat to a dish without altering its flavors.

Skate. Although skate is a delicious, abundant, inexpensive fish it has gained only marginal popularity in the States. Skate is a close cousin with rays and shares similar physical features such as the flat body flanked by two triangular fins, "wings," the only edible part of the fish. When purchasing fresh skate look for wings with the skin already removed. Fresh skate is sold in one of two ways: tender, ivory white boneless fillets or on the wing "bone," which is actually a thin piece of cartilage sandwiched in between the fillets that holds the delicate flesh together.

About Skate. The flesh should be firm and smell sweet although you may encounter fillets with a slight ammonia odor caused by urea that skate excrete through their skin. Placing the skate in an hour-long milk bath or mild acidic soak of 3 parts water to 1 part vinegar (substitute lime or lemon juice) will help cleanse the fish of excess urea and remove any odors before cooking.

Smoked Paprika. Although not a new spice, smoked paprika is a recent discovery in my kitchen that I have eagerly incorporated into Filipino-American cooking. Many of us are familiar with paprika—finely ground capsicums native to South America—that range in flavor from sweet to hot. Produced primarily in Hungary and Spain, papri-

ka is used to season and color foods. Smoked paprika, primarily from Spain, goes through an extra processing step that adds an amazing flavor boost to regular paprika. The peppers are slowly smoked over oak ash before being ground into a fine powder. The final result is paprika with a spicy, smoky, right-off-the-grill flavor that one of my colleagues succinctly described as all natural "vegetarian bacon." To find smoked paprika, look in local gourmet markets. You can also purchase it from Penzeys.com (see page 175).

Soy Sauce (*Toyo*). Soy is Asia's version of salt. This essential brown liquid is extracted from soybeans that have been fermented with mold cultures, wheat flour, and brine. There are different grades of soy, ranging from light to dark to sweet. Light soy is the saltiest of the three, the lightest in color, and the type of soy most used in our recipes. Dark soy is a milder soy based on the same ingredients as light soy but finished with caramel and matured for a longer period of time. Both light and dark soy are used for cooking as well as in dipping sauces. Sweet soy, also called sweet sauce, is a molasses-thick condiment sweetened with palm sugar. It is most often used as a dip or condiment for meats, poultry, and spring rolls.

Sweet Chili Sauce. This reddish-orange translucent sauce is a wonderful dipping accompaniment for meats, poultry, or egg rolls. Made with red chiles, sugar, vinegar, and garlic, sweet chili sauce has an excellent balance of sweet and sour flavors with a mild kick from the chiles. This prepared sauce is available in bottles but is certainly easy enough to make from ingredients that you may already have in your cupboard. (A recipe for this sauce is included on page 18.)

Tamarind. Tamarind is the pod-shaped fruit of the tamarind tree. The pod contains hard seeds in a thick brown pulp that is both sugary and intensely sour. It is very versatile as a souring agent in beverages, soups, and marinades in place of sour citrus fruits. At the grocery store, you will find tamarind in different forms: densely pressed blocks of pulp and seeds; fresh, whole pods; or liquid tamarind concentrate. If you don't use tamarind often and need only a little for a particular recipe I recommend using whole dried pods, which allow you to purchase only what you need for your dish. The pods also keep indefinitely when stored in a cool dry place. The brown pods are between 4 to 6 inches (10 to 15 cm) long and ½ to 1 inch (1 to 2½ cm) in diameter. The pods have three components: the shell, pulp, and seeds, although only the pulp is used for flavoring. The outer brown shell breaks away to reveal a single piece of tacky pulp that protects the seeds. To make **tamarind juice** soak the pulp in hot water at a ratio of 1 tablespoon pulp (approximately 2 pods) per ½ cup (125 ml) hot water. After 5 to 10 minutes the pulp will soften. Pour your tamarind and water through a fine sieve and firmly knead the pulp in the strainer to extract the tamarind juice. Discard the pulp and seeds. Other convenient forms of tamarind are compressed blocks of pulp and seeds or ready-made tamarind concentrate in liquid form. Cut the tamarind block into small 1-inch (2½-cm) blocks and freeze them for convenient use. Tamarind blocks can be soaked and pressed as you would the pod pulp to extract tamarind juice. Liquid tamarind concentrate will keep for several months in the refrigerator.

Thai Chile (*Sili Labuyo*). Also called bird peppers, these pinky-sized peppers start off green and redden upon ripening. They are extremely hot and used to add heat to any type of dish. The leaves are commonly used in Filipino cuisine wilted into soups, sautés, or stews.

Tinapa. Adding flavor and nutrition to bland food was never so easily achieved than with *tinapa*, or brined smoked fish. A common ingredient found readily in both fine restaurants and modest food stalls, tinapa's unique blend of ash and ocean are an irresistible accompaniment to any dish. Different fish are used for tinapa, including milkfish, tilapia, mackerel, bonito, and sardines. The process begins with a brine for the fish to soak in, then the fish are lightly boiled and using sawdust from the native Narra tree to lend its unforgettable aroma and golden color. You'll find smoked tinapa packaged in vacuum-sealed pouches in the refrigerated fish section of your Asian market.

Vinegar. In Filipino recipes souring agents are not necessarily used to make a dish sour but to give it added dimension and a distinct explosion of flavor. In this collection, when I list vinegar in a recipe, I'm referring to any of the Filipino vinegars listed below. Each one is an all-purpose vinegar and all but coconut palm vinegar have an acetic acid level between 4 and 5 percent. Admittedly, finding them will more than likely warrant a trip to the Asian market, but commonly available vinegars such as white distilled and cider vinegar are more acidic than Filipino vinegar and cannot be substituted without changing the amount listed in the recipe. Instead, use rice wine vinegar for an exact substitution.

Coconut Vinegar. This is an all-purpose, everyday vinegar. It is cloudy white vinegar made from the fermented coconut water collected from the center of the mature fruit. It is mild in acidity with a slightly sweet finish.

Coconut Palm Vinegar. Also a popular vinegar in Filipino cuisine, made from the fermented sap of the coco-nut palm's inflorescence. It has a slightly foggy translucence and has a low acidity ranging from 3 to 6 percent.

Nipa Palm Vinegar. Also a common all-purpose vinegar, it is made from the fermented sap of the nipa palm's inflorescence. It has a cloudy white color and is mild in acidity. It's mellow flavor makes it excellent for salad dressings or dipping sauces.

Sugar Cane Vinegar. Made from fermented sugar cane syrup, sugar cane vinegar is milder than palm or coconut vinegars and has a light amber color.

Water Spinach (*Kangkong*). This prolific Southeast Asian aquatic plant is not related to spinach but earns its name from its home on top of lakes, ponds, and rivers. The long green leaves are shaped like 5 to 6-inch (12-½ to 15-cm) arrowheads and the vinelike stems are hollow. When you're looking for kangkong at the market, you may run into two different varieties: one with thin, dart-shaped, quill-length leaves and the other with wide broad leaves, similar in shape to the sweet potato plant. Both varieties will have the characteristic hollow stems that are prized for its firm crispy texture. Look for bright green leaves free from blemishes. Kangkong has a mild flavor and can be enjoyed fresh or cooked in the same manner as regular spinach, sautéed or wilted.

Unfortunately, kangkong leaves have a short shelf life and will only last a few days at most in the refrigerator. To maximize its freshness, pick the leaves off the stems and store them separately in food storage bags. Because the stems stay fresh longer, if you don't get around to using the leaves, you can still enjoy the stems in a stir-fry or sauté as you would asparagus, green beans, or pea pods.

thechoppingblock.net. The Chopping Block is a nonprofessional cooking school and retail store in Chicago that carries a generous number of Asian and Spanish ingredients used in these recipes. They do not have a catalog or an online store, but they do ship anywhere in the United States. E-mail: info@thechoppingblock.net Store Locations: (1) 4747 N. Lincoln Avenue, Chicago, IL 60625; Tel: (773) 472-6700; (2) The Merchandise Mart Plaza, Suite 107, Chicago, IL 60654; Tel: (312) 644-6360

pilipinomart.com. This is a terrific Web site when shopping specifically for Filipino ingredients. There are pictures to help with your shopping and they offer discounts if you order in bulk. E-mail: info@pilipinomart.com; Tel: (866) 627-4956

templeofthai.com. They have a fine selection of ingredients, including those that are not just used in Southeast Asian cookery, such as noodles, sauces, and curries. What I really like about this site is that they offer some fresh items that might be difficult to find without an Asian store nearby, such as fresh galangal, lemongrass, kaffir lime leaves, and chiles. There is a minimum order of $35 delivery. E-mail: customerservice@templeofthai.com; Tel: (877) 811-8773

asianfoods.com. There is a product list on this Web site that includes a wide variety of dried and canned goods, frozen seafood, noodles, and cookware. You can also call for a free catalog. Store Locations: (1) 1300 L'Orient Street, St. Paul, MN 55117; Tel: 1-800-ASIAN55; (2) 1232 Vernon Street, N. Kansas City, MO 64116; Tel: 1-877-ASIAN57

asiafoods.com. This Web site is very user friendly with a handy shopping cart, ingredients in neat categories, and attached pictures to help you choose your products. They also have free UPS delivery for orders over $75. E-mail: info@asiafoods.com; Tel: (877) 902-0841

asianwok.com. This Web site is organized into three departments: the market, recipes, and gifts. It features foods, gifts, and recipes from China, India, Japan, Korea, and Southeast Asia. E-mail: customerservice@asianwok.com

thephilippinefoodstore.com. This Florida-based store has a Web site with contact information only (no online shopping is available), which requires you to already know what you'd like to purchase. The customer service representatives are friendly and helpful and they will ship both dry and fresh groceries to anywhere in the United States. E-mail: philippine8510@yahoo.com Store location: 8510 State Rd. 52, Hudson, FL 34667 Tel: (727) 697-3280

filgoods.com. This site offers Filipino dry goods, movies, magazines, and books. It is arranged into product categories and allows the shopper to browse by brand name. E-mail: filgoods@filgoods.com

etindahan.com. This is the Web store for the Pearl of the Orient markets in Livonia, Michigan. The Web site offers an easy to navigate selection of grocery and beauty and health goods, Filipino music, and videos.

Store Locations: (1) Pearl of the Orient, 31160 Five Mile Rd., Livonia, MI 48154; Tel: (734) 466-9999; (2) 2829 Coolidge Hwy., Berkley, MI 48072; Tel: (248) 548-0600

pacificrimgourmet.com. This site offers a global selection of gourmet foods, cookware, cookbooks, and gifts from Asia, the Pacific Islands, Mexico, and Peru. Although the Philippines inventory is not extensive, you'll find many of the basic ingredients here: dried noodles, vinegars, sauces, and spice mixes. E-mail: customerservice@pacificrim-gourmet.com

importfood.com. Despite the fact that is an online Thai market, you'll find many of the ingredients you'll need for Filipino cookery. It offers a generous selection of sauces, pastes, and canned goods as well as interesting Thai cookware and serving wares. This is also one of the three sites listed that offers a limited selection of fresh produce for shipment. E-mail: info@importfood.com; Tel: (888) 618-8424

penzeys.com. Penzeys Spices has nearly thirty retail stores nationwide and a very friendly online store. You can order spices from their catalog or the Web site. One feature that I particularly like about Penzeys Spices is that many of the spices are offered in small trial-size containers. Some are offered at quantities less than an ounce all the way up to several cups. Tel: (800) 741-7787

ACKNOWLEDGMENTS

Through this long, challenging, wonderful process one person has given me the strength and support to bring this book to life, my husband, Cesar. Thank you for all the invaluable roles you've played during the writing phase as recipe taster, dishwasher, shopper, photography assistant, and proofreader. Most of all, thank you for taking this path with me and holding my hand along the way. I also must thank my family, especially my mom and dad, Elizabeth and Jesus, and all my aunts who have given me lifelong culinary inspiration from their own kitchens. Of course, none of this would be possible without the guidance and support of my publisher. Thank you to all at Tuttle Publishing for creating a book that exceeded my expectations. I'd especially like to thank Ed Walters for recognizing the potential in this little known, yet amazing, cuisine; Courtney Nolan, my first editor, for walking me through the early stages of the process; and senior editor Holly Jennings, for your patience and expertise, and for really understanding the spirit of the book. Thank you for getting knee-deep into the material and for asking great questions.

I owe thanks to others who have lent their expertise and passion to this book. A special thanks goes to my dearest friend and sister-in-spirit, Annie Ozer, whose time and toil creating a stunning design for the preliminary book nearly equaled mine in writing it. Joaquin Soler, thanks for your help and organization in the early stages of recipe testing. Michael Lande, thank you for your amazing eye and for capturing the smell, taste, and feel of the food in your photographs. Brian Briggs Photography, thank you for putting a beautiful face to the recipes and ingredients. Dan Scesnewicz, thank you for being my sommelier and pairing the recipes with worthy libations. Thank you to Shelly Young, Sarah Stegner-Nambiar, and Paul Kahan for lending your kind words of support and endorsement to the book.

I'd also like to acknowledge the work of other writers who have focused on the Philippines, and whose books were fundamental to my research by providing me with different and exciting perspectives: Doreen Fernandez and Edilberto Alegre's *Kinilaw: A Philippine Cuisine of Freshness*, Antonio de Morga and J. S. Cummins' *Sucesos de las Islas Filipinas*, and David Joel Steinbert's *The Philippines: A Singular and a Plural Place*.

Finally, I'd like to thank my family and friends for their support and blessings. My siblings, Elissa and Ken, were always there to lend a hand or an ear. And finally, I'd like to thank my muse/daughter, Lena Aranas Casillas, for being my daily inspiration.